This is the need that changes everything: a return to center.

A return to center means rediscovering that you are both the spark and the void. It means embracing the truth of the cosmos and of life. Honoring its implications and becoming anew. It is a transformative process, like cultivating the physical body through exercise, or healing the mind from constant distraction. It means uprooting from the illusions that are so much of everyday life, and re-mooring in the soft waters of the cosmos. Becoming deeply rooted in the first living principle that winds through you. Learning to listen, and going from there.

This is what it means to live deeply.

~

Pedro Tofua

RETURNING

TO

CENTER

passages for reconnecting with the spirit, changing the world, and becoming who you're meant to be

ISBN 979-8-218-57986-9 (paperback first edition)
ISBN 979-8-9922784-0-8 (e-book)

First Paperback Edition: March 2025

Printed in the United States of America.

Mel Vie Books
6955 Willow Street NW
PMB 288
Washington, DC 20012

Title and Byline Font: Lineal by Frank Adebiaye, with the contribution of Anton Moglia, Ariel Martín Pérez. Distributed by velvetyne.fr.

Subtitle Font: Paste by Tapiwanashe Sebastian Garikayi. Distributed by stype foundry.

Cover Design by the author with contribution from visual artist JH.

Library of Congress Control Number: 2024927415

CHAPTERS AND PASSAGES

*

~

1.

A Return to Center

❋

There is a root from which all things emerge. A spark at the center of a deep void thrumming with what could and would be. From this branching, shimmering point at the heart of the cosmos, emerged the taproot of what today is called life. Here, now, it remains the first living principle, with roots that wind through all there is.

For most people, these roots are difficult to see. Often, they seem all but invisible. But they are the core of reality. They are what connect you to everything and everyone you will ever encounter. They are little bridges to forever, coursing with life, and memory, and god. Filled with what could be but never was, and what hasn't been but might still be.

These are the roots of emergence, and the roots of life. And these roots harbor not only the physical resonance of the cosmos, but its spiritual resonance. Their first movement—of living spark in living void—formed the fabric of the vibrance on the other side of life's physical matter.

Rootedness is the better question behind every question. The springing-point of each reality you find yourself in. Of each question that beats in your heart. Of each history that repeats itself.

These roots have always pulled me. From a very young age, they called from beneath a trench of grief that adults in my life struggled to understand. They made themselves known again and again as I grew. Each time I listened—and each time, I let it be as it was. Because for a growing child, what is spiritual epiphany, or unexplained phenomena, if not every-day life?

Over time, I came to understand what it meant. When it happened, it wasn't a single moment. It was a coming together of many smaller threads—a stepping back from something that's been brewing for a long time and seeing, almost suddenly, that it is done. A spiritual emergence.

And I came to understand how, across time, and across history, only a partial story of life has been told. Whether of creation, or spontaneous expansion, each version gets at some aspect, some basic truth of the cosmos.

But each version is also just that: a version. A fragment that fails to recognize what the roots of life mean for each living being. What they can offer and teach in everyday life. The profound insights in the simple fact of where we come from—and the promise of learning to understand them.

And because today, so many people, especially young people, draw their understanding of the world and of life from fragments of something much older, and much more profound, many are left unmoored. So many of us are left afloat, and without center.

Like a planet that's lost its orbit and is now adrift in a system, untethered from the sun that grounds and guides and gives life. Without that steady orbit, without the clarifying vitality of the star that pulls it, without the balance of spark and void that create the conditions for life, a world cannot be full and lush and alive. It cannot transform or grow.

And that is the state so many people find themselves in. A state that gets so familiar, it starts to feel like life.

Maybe surrounded, but often still lonely. Maybe busy, but often without meaning. Maybe inspired, but far from the life and world they could be living in.

This is the need that changes everything: a return to center.

A return to center means rediscovering that you are both the spark and the void. It means embracing the truth of the cosmos and of life. Honoring its implications and becoming anew. It is a transformative process, like cultivating the physical body through exercise, or healing the mind from constant distraction. It means uprooting from the illusions that are so much of everyday life, and re-mooring in the soft waters of the cosmos. Becoming deeply rooted in the first living principle that

13

winds through you. Learning to listen, and going from there.

This is what it means to live deeply.

~

Now

It's those moments. The longing at the edge of the forced smile. The loneliness that doesn't visit but overwhelms. The deeper truth that seems just out of reach, on the other side of the feeling that this can't be all there is.

That's what it is to float through life. To be lost, to miss the tether that would otherwise hold you.

It's in that question, what am I even doing?

It's in that sibling feeling, who am I?

That frequent visitor, why am I here?

Each one is a manifestation of a deeper detachment, a deeper disconnect, and stems from something much deeper than the self, or any single identity, or any one choice.

Too often, the world will offer you "healing" that doesn't address the root. It will offer ideas that encourage you to turn inwards or endure until your time is up, with a promise about what comes next. But, in doing so, those same ideas forget that you are here, now, for a reason. In a search for answers, you'll find philosophy that encourages you to transcend or untether, but in encouraging this it forgets your place in the living whole. It's not always easy to see, but all of these make it worse.

Because the problem *is* a lack of tethering, a lack of immersion, a lack of connection with all there is and your unlikely place in it. The problem is an unmooring from the forever that brought and birthed and keeps you here. From the force that fills you now, in this life, and connects you to the cosmos, always.

And it's those moments—the search for the role of others in your life, and you in theirs. Of where you belong and who you can become. Of how your life can be, how the world can be, and how to get there. Those moments all stem from a similar disconnect: a lost bond to the roots of life. Lost keys to transformation—to moving from one reality to a different one.

But there was a time once, a place, where these questions, feelings, and moments were intentionally navigated. Where the realm of the spirit was seen as a pillar of society—like any other form of knowledge, or way of living.

This way of being produced a deep understanding of not only who each person was, but of each person's purpose and place in the world. And beyond. A deep understanding of each person's connection to all things, and each person's paths in this lifetime.

This was the first way. Not that it had a name, then, but this is the most fitting way to describe it. The first way was the way of the grandparents of my great-great-grandparents. It taught people about, and prepared them for, life and living. It empowered each person to fulfill their roles in this life, and in the lives of others. And at its center, was depth.

But over many years, this knowledge was stripped, and its history omitted. It became one of the deepest and most underexplored casualties of an injustice that today still stains the human psyche. And the same injustice left the world without a frame to even understand what it lost.

Without that rootedness, without that deeper knowledge, there is little way to know that all this could be different—and that the answers to so many of those forever questions have been with you since before you were born.

That's why this book exists.

This book is a song of the spirit. It's the story of something lost, with everything to teach. Of something given freely, but easily missed in the lonely noise of everywhere you go.

It's a new verse in an ancient song. It's a continuation of a first movement, played from the core. Something channeled from the ocean of all things—the churning, cosmic energy that courses through each of us and all of us. In its own way. A song from the spark that, in you, gains a cosmic fingerprint. Where soul becomes spirit. It is a song from there. Written because it demanded to be, shared in case you need it. It's mine to share with you.

Doing this justice has been more than a deep reflection. It's been a devoted ritual of unearthing. A listening. A calling. May you read it as such.

This is a book for reading often. Not with your eyes, but with all your being. With how you breathe and dream and move through the world. Reflect with it and reflect on it. As in life, each chapter stands both alone and together with the rest of the whole. Explore it as you will. Take note and let your mind wander. Then come back and give it more. Go to the deepest depths, and then go further. Inhale. Exhale. Begin again.

In here you'll find hues of life and spirit. You'll find some history, and some artistry. Some questions, more answers. Above all, you will find truths; to be considered, explored, and reveled in. To be lived.

Because that is what this book—what the song of the spirit—is for. Living. May you live it fully.

~

A reminder of everything

There is, in some places, a knowing. You may have felt it. On quiet nights or mornings. By the sea or with the trees or under the stars, in the great temples of life. A glimpse of everything. The depths of truth.

This knowing bears answers to many things that matter. The "why" of life. And the "why" of your life. What the world needs from you, and what you need. What should be done about it. Where you come from and where you're going and where it all fits. What's broken, and how to mend it.

It's a knowing that can be traced on a thread, tens of thousands of years old, to southern Africa. Where all human life on this planet emerged. Where my own ancestors stewarded this knowing for millennia, until it became a painful casualty of colonization. Today, it's a knowing that lives and grows. It is born and reborn in its bearers, and it lingers in rich philosophical traditions that could never be completely quelled—because truth is difficult to silence.

Echoes of this knowing can be found across many different spiritual traditions of the world. You might notice their themes in traditions as varied as those of the ancient Celts to the origins of Hinduism. But this is something wholly its own, and often much older.

Be mindful—this is not something to be "borrowed," or adopted or selectively applied. Its teaching does not belong to everyone. But its truth is real for all. It deals not only with earth, but with the cosmos. Not just with the mind, but with the spirit. To know it is to have a pathway to everything. To live it is to be true. This is an invitation to learn, to revere, and to embark. If you choose to, come humbly. Be responsible, be real, and be open. Immerse.

First, there's an end. Everything that ever lived was born from something else. Each fiber of your skin. Each hair growing from its crevices. Each breath you take in, and each beat in your chest. It is here because of what came before. And even now, it's pregnant with what's to come.

The same is true of the cosmos. The planets that come from stars. The stars that are born from nebulae. The nebulae that emerge from remnants of stars that lived before.

All begin as dust. All return to dust. And from dust all begin. Birth to peak to death to dust. And then birth again.

This process—this cycle—is the first great constant of life.

Too often, this cycle is ignored.

It's ignored when you move too quickly away from something that hurts. When you don't allow time to feel what needs to be felt. When a person is too certain in themselves or too quick to admonish others.

That's why it's important to go deeply into all things you do and feel and to be with them a while. To revisit what you assume or take for granted and embrace the things that are true at their core. To be full because of the space you fill for others, and because of the small and deep space you fill in the broader cosmos. This is what it means to live.

It's also a cycle that's true of every society, but not all societies respect it. When societies respect it, they thrive. When they don't, they inevitably give way to what comes next. The longer the arrogance, the worse the outcome.

Remember: transient pain is a part of life, but systemic pain is a symptom of something broken.

A society that prioritizes destruction and dominance and punishment destroys itself, in the end. A society that prioritizes extraction, consumption, and production eats until there is nothing left to eat.

The society that prioritizes life, harmony, fulfillment, will find itself alive, harmonious, and fulfilled. The natural state of things is regeneration. Regeneration does not require assistance. It only asks to be honored, and to be heeded.

To know the spirit, to know each other, to know life—these are sacred. Nature is not a place you visit, but a being that lives inside you. Life is not random, but a gift and a charge set out before you arrived in these bones. The spirit is as powerful a force as that of gravity and radio waves and ultraviolet light. It works through our world. Collectively, it lives in you, as you live in it. It's plainly there, awaiting not revelation, but acknowledgment. It is always with you, and you are always with it.

But when you become untethered from it, as many are, things no longer make sense. Life no longer bears fruit. And health, wealth, and luck are hard to come by.

To live in spirit is to live in truth. And it is to have health, wealth, and luck.

Truth is in the wind in the trees, and in the whispers of your memory. In the folds of your skin, and the hairs that grow between them. In the spirits of the earth, and in the ocean of our ancestors. Inside you and around you and before you and after. To ignore it, to live against it, is the greatest lie of all.

God is not hidden, waiting for you to die. God is everywhere, urging you to live. Will you listen?

~

Death

Death marks the end of one thing and the beginning of another. All life moves through a thousand tiny, daily deaths. Growth itself is a process of death. From the dead hair cells that shed and give way to new ones, to the trees born from the ashes of wildfire. It should not be feared, but respected. And it should not be "overcome" or ever "moved on from." It should be lived.

Grief is a powerful force. A supernova. A monument to something lost, and a reminder of what remains. A reminder of lifetimes.

There is often an urge to move on from grief. A pressure from others, or a codification in society. But while it's good and healthy for grief to eventually fade, the bond does not. Love does not. Memory does not. And each of them should not.

When a death occurs, the relationship with the passing person does not end—it evolves. The person who dies becomes unwound from this physical world. But their spirit endures, with a root here for so long as someone living nurtures it, for so long as the person is memorialized. And the living energy which once coursed through them passes on to the great cosmic ocean from which all living energy comes. And the cycle continues.

~

Cycles of life: the four stages

To live is to move through cycles. Cycles of change. Cycles of desire. Cycles of being. It is to follow four stages, echoed across the cosmos from the life cycle of a star to that of a cell.

Standing on a beach somewhere, where the water comes from the east, you can see the top half of the sun emerging from the water's distant edge. It slathers the waning night in gold and copper, red and violet. This is dawn, the first stage.

The sun then rises, in an arc, until it stands tall above the water, the sand, the clouds. It stretches its rays until it's its brightest, its warmest, its most visible. This is peak day, the second stage.

Satisfied, the sun begins its descent towards the horizon. It nestles into that first position, half over half under the water's line, a world away from where it began, falling in the west where it rose in the east. This is dusk, the third stage.

Even falling below the water, as dusk gives way to night, the sun's journey continues.

When the sun crosses this boundary, it completes its mirror arc, in the darkness. Setting here, somewhere it rises. Beneath the water, it moves now back towards the center, until it sits directly beneath where it stood at high noon, or peak day. In this place, it is midnight—the fourth stage. And the fourth stage is not the end.

Because then, the sun begins its rise towards that morning east. Towards the dawn. And the cycle continues, on, and on.

There are several places on earth where this cycle isn't daily. At certain times of year, the arctic regions, for example, see long nights, and long days—lasting more than 24 hours—what's sometimes called polar night, or polar day, respectively. The cycle here is the same, with longer stages. This is the first hidden truth of the cycle: it's not equal parts always. Stages vary. From being to being, and moment to moment, the cycle will ebb and flow and still, it will continue.

At a larger scale, the sun also doesn't move from its position at the center of the solar system. Its rise, its peak, its set, its dip below the horizon—these are, physically speaking, relative positions, made alive by the earth's constant rotation.

And this reveals the second hidden truth of the four stages of the cycle: they are not discreet, but constant. They are not absolute, but relative. Like the sun that sits and flares at the center of this star system, Life sits and flares. Stages don't really end, nor do they truly begin. The cycle moves. It is. It flows.

And this is what all life does: flow. Dawn, peak, dusk, depth.

Each cycling being affects others. Take the moon: Moonrise, peak, moonset, morning. This dance, this pirouette of the moon around our spinning planet, ripples into the tides of the sea, the rhythms of our sleep, the fertility of our bodies. Just as earth's two-step with the sun gives rise to currents, seasons, plant life, and mood swings, the moon dance also births new cycles.

If we go higher, past the moon, and return to the cosmos, we know each star follows this same pattern. A birth from dust. A rise, over billions of years, through a typical form like that of our sun, to eventually peak (as a red giant or supergiant). A cooling period leading to the death of its prior form, or a loss of stability leading to a supernova. Returning to the depths (as a black hole or nebula). Begin again.

The universe itself, while subdivided into different numbers of eras by different astrophysicists, can be described as following these four stages. Birth, peak, set, return. And again.

The omniverse, the term sometimes used to describe the set of all possible universes, where it's assumed there exist multiple, does the same.

The earth and its sister planets, too, bear this cosmic DNA. Birth, peak, change, return.

Inside you, the cosmos repeats itself in your cells. Preparation, synthesis, organization, division. While you can subdivide these further, at its most basic, the cell cycle follows the same cycles of life.

Which leads to you. Physically, the cycle is clear. First breath, adulthood, death, return to earth. Here, perhaps, is where the fluid constancy is clearest. You do not simply breathe and then stand. You do not simply stand and then walk. You are not simply born and then an adult.

Rather, you move from rest to first breath. From first breath to first crawl. From first crawl to first step. From first step to walking. From walking to running. From running to walking. From walking to sitting. From sitting to rest. And the breath, too, moves.

But all this happens above that horizon line. All this is first light to last. There exists, physically, a night. And it is within the earth.

You came from parents who ate the earth to nourish your bones, your skin, your body. Here, you were in the depths. You live. You eat. When you die, physically, you return to the earth, and it eats you back. The compounds of your body merge with the land that feeds and gives rise to life in new parents. This is why it's important to be buried. Because when you take the body in the context of the world from which it came, you see that you are already immortal. This is the peace you find when you embrace the cycle of all things.

Your spirit, too, follows the cycle.

Before you are a body, you are a spirit. After you are a body, you are a spirit. When the cosmic, living energy that permeates all things is allocated to a life, a soul is born. Just as the mind is born with the body, the spirit is born with the soul. Consciousness the bridge between them.

The soul rises in this life. It lives. The soul then sets in this life. And, once it sets here, it rises again into the place from which it came. There, it eventually loses its living character, the spirit, and becomes, again, cosmos. Until it rises again here, and is given new character. And in this way, it goes and comes and goes and comes again.

Like the body returns to the earth, the spirit returns to the depths. Like the body eventually *becomes* earth and nourishes physical life, the spirit eventually becomes soul and nourishes spiritual life.

Both lose their forms and gain new ones. Both go from being concentrated in a person, to deconstructing and adjoining with the great beyond. The body lives a lifetime, but in the earth it lives millennia. The spirit lives for generations, and, in the cosmos, much longer.

The best life is long and healthy, and each part of the cycle, no matter how long, receives its due. When the cycle is interrupted, through unnatural violence or through disease, a tragedy has occurred. The best way to reduce these instances isn't just personal, but social. It's important to create *societies* which prevent unnatural violence and avoid disease. Because every being is entitled to a full and natural life.

The best life ends, one day, allowing the cycle to continue. While some are desperate to live forever, it is important, in due time, to leave these lifetimes behind, so that we and the rest may continue on. Life feeds one part of the world, and death another. This balance, just as with day and night, push and pull—is the great wave of existence.

Our bodies are outlived by our memory. Our memory is outlived by our spirit. Our spirit is outlived by the cosmos from which we came, in which we are entangled, and with which we are imbued. This is the cycle of life.

~

The nature of Mind and Spirit

The mind is your body's identity while you are here. The body is the physical piece of cosmos, your own microcosm of earth, the living leaf on the tree of life. The spirit is your soul's identity. The soul is the little piece of the cosmos, the living energy, which imbues everything in that deeper plane of existence. It is the crackle and spark from a wildfire. The droplet in a wave of the ocean. The coil of hair on the tenth arm of god.

All of these are you and yours. But they are not only you, and not only yours.

When you go, you lose your mind to time, and your body to the earth. Your spirit remains a while. One day, it too fades back into the cosmic sea of all things, and, having lived well, returns to the cosmic center, the heart of light that links all souls. It brings with it what it became—the ugly dissonance or the beautiful harmony that marked your life and deeds. That cosmic sea continues to churn, and swell, and ease. And the cycle remains.

~

Of purpose and promise

What you should do with your life. Why you're here. Why it matters. These questions are common today, because there's been a great untethering. An untethering from that deeper world, that deeper knowledge, moored in the fabric of our being.

Today's society asks people, especially young people, to trade off between comfort and survival, the future and the present, themselves and others. Over many years, the value of deep thought, the value of honest, messy, nuanced connection—the value of living fully—have been eroded. And rather than asking how to live well, people are left wondering why to live at all.

The question of purpose is fundamental. But it's gotten lost in ideas that only pretend to be answers. What job or major to have. How much schooling to pursue. How to be liked or followed. How to win, do, get. All valuable, in some way. But nothing to do with the reason you're here.

Purpose is not about the things you use to gain something else.

Purpose is a calling out from the worlds that could be to the world we walk through. Purpose is an unfilled need that addresses itself by concentrating physical, experiential, and cultural possibilities in a person. Purpose is the compass that guides and the star that leads. It is a nudge from the cosmos, and a promise to the world.

Your purpose is clear as day. In common with the waves and the leaves and the stars. Written in the sand and fragrant in the breeze. Obvious, when you stop for a moment to listen.

Your purpose is to live.

The real question is not what your purpose is, but what your promise is. Not "who you are," but who you can and should be. Not what to do with your life, but how to live well. How to understand your roles in the great cosmic tapestry. How to shed what slowly kills, and cultivate what enlivens. How to hear who you are called to be, and become so.

Because when you become so, when you live well, when you understand your promise and live up to it, a resonant note is played in the cosmic song. A harmony is unearthed, a gift is given, and you become a conduit for seeds of a reality that wants to exist. You become as you were always meant, but not certain, to be. And the world opens.

~

2.

The collective spirit and the need for repair

❋

There is often a narrative that tells you about the importance of *you*. The individual struggle to be an individual. The call to separate yourself from a larger system that wants to stifle uniqueness. It's a narrative that is deeply broken.

Imagine you're walking, deep in the forest. You come across a tree that grabs your attention; beautiful, gnarled branches and slithering ivy. You stop and look at this tree for a while—it draws you. And then you move on.

Is the tree not a marvel? Yes, it is. Is there any tree exactly like it? No. But is it not also a tree, in a forest full of trees? Is it not also one part (tree) of a whole (forest)? And even then, is it not one whole (tree) of many parts (leaves, trunk, branches, roots)? Is not each leaf one whole of many cells, themselves wholes of many organelles... Each forest one part of many forests, themselves one part of a whole (earth)...

Because the truth is, individuality and collectiveness are two perspectives on the same reality. They are useful distinctions, but they are not fundamentally different.

In this same way, your spirit is one whole part of a collective spirit. When it aches, so too does the collective. And when the collective ails, so too does your own spirit. To believe or not believe in justice, to believe or not believe in the need to heal not only individuals, but the collective, does not change the reality that plagues the spirit where the role of the collective, the wrongness of injustice, or the echoes of harm across time and space are overlooked, ignored, or forcibly repressed.

Social repair is not just a lofty ideal, it is an existential imperative.

When one tree is on fire, you do not ignore it assuming the fire only affects the tree. You recognize that fire spreads. You understand that the smoke fumes can be deadly to everything that breathes. You tend to the fire not thinking only of the single tree, but of the whole forest. The care for life, and for people, is the same. In looking to heal one person, look also to what is unhealed in the collective.

Because sometimes, the forest is sick. Sometimes that sickness gives birth to deformed or parasitic systems of life. And for healing to be possible, sometimes there is first an entrenched ugliness, a sickness, that must be removed from the trees. And the networks that keep the illness alive in the forest must be snuffed out.

In looking to address and redress past or present harm, or become all that you can, or contribute to healing in the world or in your own life, bear in mind that transformation sometimes calls for fire—the movement of the spirit, personal and collective, from one state to another. The slow and honest process of making ashes of what was, and planting, then cultivating, what could be.

New things are born in fire. For the collective and for the individual.

But fire is also dangerous. Without understanding the roots of a problem, any proposed solution will create more problems. So, take time, first, to understand the origins of the forest, and the ailments that plague it. Begin with history, and with reverence for life. Begin with care, and the humility of inherited experience. And from there seek repair.

~

The paradigm of the South

Often, if you walk into a bookstore and approach the spiritual or philosophy section, you'll see a diverse selection of teachings.

In one section, you may find lessons on transcendence, meditation, and escape from suffering. Ideas of duality and flow. Philosophies that focus on interconnectedness, rather than individuality. And they will have a lot to teach. These are the paradigms of the East.

Still, in other stores and sections, you will find everything from popular science and guides to the self, to astrology, typology, and mastery. Ideas of stoicism, objectivity, and independence. Philosophies that focus on individuality, rather than interconnectedness. These are the paradigms of the West.

And those who study religions will notice the body of academic religious knowledge operates on a distinct East-West spectrum as well. Either the modern ideals of the West (with roots in Judeo-Christianity), the Taoic and Dharmic traditions of the East (Buddhism, Taoism, Hinduism(s), etc.), or the other Abrahamic or parallel traditions of the middle (Islam, Zoroastrianism, etc.).

But the East-West paradigm is not all there is. In fact, it misses one of the most important pieces of human history, and is a core reason why so much of our shared body of spiritual knowledge is incomplete today. Because many well-known traditions—from the practices now described as "pagan" found throughout Europe that reemerged later in North America, to the hidden, often syncretic customs carried on in Brazil and Haiti and Louisiana—are great-grandchildren of an original, ancient knowledge with deep roots in southern Africa. Not only does this ancient knowledge have much to teach today's world, not only is it the birthright of each of its descendants, but it's a part of the story of every person on this planet.

The first modern humans on Earth emerged more than 200,000 years ago in what is today Sub-Saharan Africa. That is, the region south of the Sahara Desert in Africa. Some alternative theories of human movement suggest this happened even earlier—that the precursor to modern humans emerged in Africa over 1.5 million years ago, traveling and establishing (or joining) human settlements elsewhere. To put this in perspective, the first Europeans arrived in Africa less than 1,000 years ago, Jesus is said to have walked less than 3,000 years ago, and the pyramids of Egypt were built less than 5,000 years ago. The history below is concerned with the more than 195,000 years of human life before that, and with what can be learned from places and people that today are less discussed.

Over tens of thousands of years, the people of Sub-Saharan Africa, organized in part by shared languages, came to comprise what many scholars today commonly refer to as the Khoisan and Atlantic-Congo language families. But the world's African and Afro-descendant peoples have always been more than the languages they speak or skin they share—we are an extended family with deep, shared roots and varied, diverse cultures.

Today, this family of people represents many hundred native ethnic groups, and more than 2,000 languages. It numbers more than the entire population of North America and spans a complex and diverse range of cultures. These are Dogon, Futa, and Yoruba. Kongo, Chokwe, Zulu, Swahili, and many, many more.

At well over 1 billion-strong, the people of this family are related to each member of the Afro-diaspora, and, in a way, they are distant relatives of every human being on earth. Because, given the shared emergence of our species in ancient southern Africa, its people are in some sense the world's first people, and the family of all. This reality is a reminder of our fundamental relationship with each other. The connection between every one of us.

And the paradigm of the South began with them—and specifically, in southern Africa. In the region of my own great ancestors, that today encompasses the nations of Angola, Botswana, Congo, Namibia, and Zambia.

Long before it was colonized, in this place we all came from, the first people understood the world as an entity to live in relationship with.

Everywhere they looked, there was life. Something to tend to. Something to give. Everything there was had a relationship with something else. And they built communities and cities with this in mind. For the people of southern Africa, the land was not a thing to own, but a home to live in. To care for. The world was not just what they could see, but the sun, the moon, the stars, the cosmos. It was, in places, assumed that there were other planets, some of which harbored life. That there were other people, in places, like humans in consciousness, but not in form. They saw the cosmic, living energy in all life, and the constancy of change. For my own great-great-grandparents, the word for god was, in places and at times, the same as the word for change.

And importantly, life was not something to escape, or to dominate, but to live up to. People were taught, from a young age, how to become all that they could be—for their community and, in turn, for themselves.

Society was considered something to be collectively shaped to become all that it should be. And nature was something not to control, but to embrace.

This is the paradigm of the South. The paradigm of the South is neither the transcendentalism of the West nor is it the transcendence of the East. It is a paradigm of water, and living, and transformation. And it is different from what might be called the paradigm of the North, which is the way of living most people are familiar with today (but don't always think about).

Where the paradigm of the North seeks knowledge through dissection, the paradigm of the South gains understanding through communion. While the paradigm of the North preferences dispassion and the material, the paradigm of the South values the physical and spiritual whole. In the northern way, the truth is within you. In the southern way, the truth is all around you. In the northern way, you are as you are. In the southern way, you become who you can be. It is a powerful difference.

And still, this first way of seeing, this first knowledge, has been omitted from common awareness.

There are many reasons for this omission. One, is that much of this knowledge was never written. It was simply known, and passed down, in spirit to those called to listen carefully, commune with, and understand it, and through the spoken word. It became an oral history, whose books are those who bear it. Were the observers of the first way to be exposed to the some of the recent discoveries of modern science—many of them might not see discoveries at all, but rather the slow learning and peculiar naming conventions of an insular group of people, laying claim to what was already known, as they stare at clouds and miss the sky.

And that's another reason for the omission of this history: inadvertent ignorance. The understanding of most people of the role of the peoples of Sub-Saharan Africa and their descendants, is as people who were enslaved, became free, and now live in poverty and struggle. Many don't seek these books or teachers out, because they don't know the extent of the history of these same people— never wondered what they were doing while their cousins in Europe and around the Mediterranean had their crusades and "Dark Ages." Never learned the role the first people have played in the story of humanity, perhaps most extensively so in the collective human understanding of life and the spirit.

Which leads to the third and most insidious reason this knowledge has been lost: destruction by design.

When various peoples of Subsahara (like their Native American cousins across the ocean) first encountered Europeans, at different points in history, often the response was the same. A welcoming, with open arms. And this was, in some ways, cultural. Among many Bantu cultures, for example, the custom of being a good host to strangers extended from the understanding of all people as part of a large, extended, human family or community. The arriving Europeans were often received as distant cousins and neighbors to be welcomed as one would a closer cousin or neighbor.

But those who came to colonize had been distant for too long. Somewhere, in the long march out of Africa and in the tens of thousands of years that followed, the ties that bound the incoming visitors to this deeper knowledge, to this crucial understanding of life and spirit, had shriveled to dust.

And so, everywhere they looked, they saw something to be taken. They looked at the verdant forest, brimming with life and shade and home, and saw something to be replaced. They looked at trees and saw only lumber. People and saw only animals. Animals and saw only beasts.

And when they saw how the people understood the land, danced with the moon, and revered the spirits—they decided the people of southern Africa were backwards and brutish. So, they coerced people to abandon the traditions, and replaced these with their own colder songs, truths, and books. They impelled people across the sea, to places where they'd done the same, and forced them to build pollutant empires in their name. They taught people to dislike their own way—of reverence, life, and abundance—and to accept a new way—of desecration and extraction.

And a system was born. One that outlived the colonizers but continues to colonize. One that has been passed down, generation to generation, through what is learned and what is not. Through what is loved, and what is not. Through whom is forgiven, and who isn't.

Because of it, a great knowledge has been lost. The great promise of humanity is under threat. And few have the lives they deserve.

This is why colonization is a great evil. Because it kills. Because it takes. Because it burdens, physically *and* spiritually. And in doing so to one group of people, it does so to all people, across time and space.

Because if the world's first people are everyone's ancestors, they are, in some way, everyone's family. What does it say about our current society, that it was built on violence and cruelty against its own family?

Today, the world is less enlightened, less whole, and less rich because of the actions of a few upon their cousins. While the people of the world's Afro-Diaspora and their Indigenous relatives across the planet have paid the steepest price, all the world is worse off.

So, as you read this book, bear in mind and heart that these truths come from there. Remember that while these words carry the heritage, the weight, and the significance of their history, they are no less true for any one person or more true for another. They simply are. Keep this, respect it, honor it as you would the greatest gift. Seek out this paradigm, and its truths, because they are as fundamental to life as any other truth.

What is written here, now, is both new and ancient. It is a specific work rooted in now, but also rooted in the paradigm of the South. The work in these pages is part of the forever story of the human spirit. It is uniquely personal, and it's also the story of us, and a story for us. All.

~

Justice and repair

When a great harm is done, it's borne not only by the harmed, but also by those who injure. Harm is done not only in the moment, but in every moment that follows without remedy. Its damage is felt a across time. Its pain is inherited, and its guilt putrefies. And the burden is passed, spiritually, and physically, to each descendant of the injured and injurer.

Violence, desecration, extraction—these leave wounds, each blow outlived by the skin it parts. The entrenchment of these in the systems that govern a society prevent the wounds, now festering, from scarring over. The society may limp on, thinking itself fine, while the whole world watches it bleed onto the ground. As it leaves crimson footprints in its wake. As it struggles to keep its limbs together, still smiling, adamant it needs nothing from, and owes nothing to, anyone.

Society is, itself, a body. And a body, injured, must be healed. Each day its wounds go unremedied, it gains new ones. As these wounds compile, the body, bruised and bloodied and infected, eventually gives out. Even if it sees the wounds, and claims there is no cure, a cure must be found.

Because it's not enough to address wounds—wounds must be redressed. It must be understood, in such a society, that all are wounded, in opposing ways. To force is to experience equal and opposite force. To injure another, is to injure yourself. And to build a society through injury, is to destroy the society that could instead be.

For as long as there is breath in a body, and vitality in its spirit, there can be healing. For as long as there is healing, there can be repair. But once begun, healing must be nurtured with time, devotion, and discipline— because it takes longer to heal than to harm.

Justice is the social poultice. It is rest and care for the injured. Mending and rejuvenation for the injurer. The poultice must be applied with care. In time, it must be cleaned, changed, and reapplied. And again. Because each wound heals slowly. And when too many wounds have accumulated, then the whole body, ill, must have time to heal as well.

Even given that time, a wound will not simply close—it will scar. The deepest wounds will mark a body its entire life. Each deep wound will take years of discipline to treat, and where properly cared for, the body will live, wounded and scarred, but whole again. And it's this honest sacrifice, devoted mending, careful nurture, that restores.

And the collective human body has seen no greater wound than the grievousness of colonialism and its progeny. Justice and repair are needed not only for those who were colonized, but for their descendants. To mend the system that continues to colonize. To restore harmony to the human spirit, knocked restless and off-kilter by impossible pain.

Because this is not an injury done once. It was done, and done again, and done again. Each act of injury more painful than the last. No attempts to mend were given the time, devotion, and discipline needed to succeed. And when evil is done, it weighs on the spirit.

When the spirit returns to soul, it brings this weight into the cosmos, disrupting the harmony of things. And so, it is passed down, in body and spirit, generation to generation, burdening those not yet given a chance to live weightless with the grave responsibility of healing. Because without redress, wounds linger and continue to worsen. And soon, the whole world breaks.

Humanity's body lives scarred and uncared for. To mend it, each people deeply wounded—in particular, the people of southern Africa, their global descendants, and the many Indigenous peoples of the world—must have physical and spiritual justice. And the injurers, equally and oppositely wounded, must see to that justice—for the injured and for them-selves. Because when we cause great harm to others, the only action that can close each equal and opposite wound that opens in our heart, each heavy weight on our spirit, is great sacrifice, great giving, and great care. Because only through justice and repair can many wounded peoples become one whole people.

All people are owed justice. True justice does not ostracize, maim, or kill. True justice does not dispossess or destroy.

True justice gives. True justice mends. True justice lasts. When they cause injury, a person must remedy it with conviction. The person must first come to understand the depth of harm that has been caused. They must then give, mend, and provide redress with discipline, devotion, and care.

A person, having committed harm, is not any less of a person. They are, instead, sick with wrongness. And the harm they do is only rectified through acts of repair. The greater the harm, the greater the acts of repair must be.

Remember also, that harm and discomfort are not the same. Often, discomfort is an important part of growth, and even of promoting justice. Justice is mediated not by belief, but by reality. By what is broken, and what needs mending.

At scale, justice is a matter of societies, not individuals. In any society, large or local, for every great harm done to a people, great repair must be secured. When time passes from when a great harm was done, the burden of great repair does not vanish—it grows and gets inherited. The longer the wait, the greater the need, until for each generation the harm deepened or went unaddressed, 4 generations are needed to set it right. And it becomes the responsibility of the inheritors to demand it.

Because a society that does not seek disciplined, devoted, careful justice is poorly led, and requires new leadership. People who avoid disciplined, devoted, and careful justice burden themselves above all, and must be led to change. Because true justice is a bridge to repair. And only through repair can the wounded body, forever scarred, be whole.

~

Society

A society is a home. It is a place that feeds or starves. A resting place, and a birthing place. The cradle of identity.

This is why whenever there's something wrong in a society, there will be something wrong with the people, and whenever there's something wrong with a person, there will be something wrong in the society.

The society is therefore the responsibility of all who live in it. Its role should be to nurture, and to protect. To adhere to life, to honesty, and to wellbeing.

Where it fails, it must be reformed. Where it harms, it must restore. Where it deceives, it must be made honest.

Sometimes, a society in which you live may warp a person's body or mind. It'll give rise in the person beliefs or attitudes which may be, at their core, dishonest. And, having found comfort in this dishonesty, the person may cling to it. Don't mistake healing with punishing a person for their predicament. Don't cast blame. Instead, change the society.

What is right in one society, may not be right in another. Don't force change in that which isn't yours. That's one path to injustice. Instead, approach difference with humility and respect. Learn where you can.

Still, there is a deeper truth that transcends place, and time. It is the truth of spirit, and the truth of life. The truth of the cycle, and its four stages. The truth of the cosmos.

For life to flourish, for worlds to thrive, for people to live according to purpose, this truth must be embedded at the heart of each society. This is your work, if you accept and observe it.

A society is smaller than a grain of sand in the desert of the cosmos. And you are a fleck on that grain. When you see only the grain of sand, it becomes your whole world. And a world is impossible to move. But when you see the desert, and understand the grain on which you sit is only one of a sandy sea, you understand your society for what it truly is.

Remember, always, that shifting dunes, the wind, and even the weight of a fleck can

61

move a grain of sand. Remember, always, to
move with the desert, and not the grain.

~

Community

People are bound by family, found and given. Families are bound by community. While it may bear communities, a society is not a community. A community arises from communion.

The community, like the body, is born. It has a spirit. It follows the cycle of all things.

The harmonious community is honest. It flows from the great cosmic tapestry. It adheres to life. And communities are the building blocks of what a society could one day be.

So don't seek community in wayward things. Don't commune with people who won't go deeper. Find community, instead, in the nourishment of life. Find it in your shared purpose with the sun and the trees and the sand. With rootedness, and with a memory of stardust. With the song of the spirit.

~

Belonging

A person belongs in their own bones. This is why you were placed in these bones: to be in them. This is why you were born in this skin. To be in it.

Too often, people want to escape their own flesh, their own mind. But the flesh and the mind are a home for the spirit while it is here. It's your work to tend them. Because only with a nurtured body and mind can the spirit find its place to flourish.

Do not run from the body you were given—instead, strengthen it. Care for it. Honor it. Do not run from the mind you were given—instead, nourish it. Keep your mind and body fit, and you will find space for the glow of your spirit.

A person, too, belongs in this world. Or the world would not have evolved for them to be here. You belong here. Not there.

Society, however, is different. Circumstance can place a person in a broken society. In a world still wounded from past injuries, any society a person comes into will be less than what it could be. Some societies much more than others. This is why it's important to create societies of life, nourishment, and abundance everywhere in the world. Because a person can be born in any one of them. It's not enough to find peace in yourself if all around you people are hurting. Society is a home. When the home is on fire, the fumes can kill, and the fire spread. It's not enough to escape the burning home. The fire must be put out.

So, remember then that a broken society needs mending. It is that mended society, that mended world, in which everyone belongs. Each generation, a world grows closer or further from being a place in which to belong. Bring it closer.

~

Leadership

Leadership is the head of the society. The character of the community. Every group, small or large, takes after its leadership. When its leadership prioritizes life, wellbeing, and harmony—a society will find itself healthy, well, and beautiful. When its leadership prioritizes accumulation, extraction, and retribution—a society will find itself obese, bereft, and hurting.

The same is true at the smallest scale.

Don't empower leaders who claim the society's best interest, but don't value its health. Don't empower leaders who claim to value life but are quick to injure it. And don't empower leaders who are quick to extract, but slow to conserve.

Good leaders are those who work to create the society where full life can thrive. Good leaders seek repair for the injured, justice for the burdened, and harmony for the living. To lead is to be the greatest servant. Cherish those who serve well. Reject those who do not.

Service isn't just giving people what they want. Service is giving a society what it needs. A good leader serves well when the leader enlivens the spirit of a society or community. A good leader serves well when they lead their group(s) to life, honesty, and wellbeing. To justice and to harmony. To the reality all people deserve.

It's not the number of leaders that matters. A society with many bad leaders will be led badly. A society with one good leader will be led well. A democracy with a public that is poorly suited will crumble as quickly as a monarchy with a wayward queen or king. Leaders don't have a thousand eyes— necessary to serve millions of people—and so they must have good advisors—spiritual and physical. Meanwhile, the public is easily misled, made foolish, and turned quick to condemn—three traits of poor leadership. Therefore, the public must always have good leadership, from among its wisest.

Very few are truly called to lead. And this is good, because the burden of leadership is too much for all, or even most, people in a place to bear.

But it is a burden, and it must be borne.

When the burden falls on your shoulders, bear it wisely, and dutifully. When it must fall on the shoulders of others, hold them up so they may bear it well. The person called to lead *becomes* a leader, each day, or they fail to.

Leadership is a living force. Like all living forces, it passes and comes. It is a state of being. A leader can lead in some places, and follow in others. It doesn't matter how long they lead—it matters how often they lead well. The mark of a good leader is not how much they want to have, but how much they want to give. It's in what they want to see in the world, for the world; the vitality of their vision for the society they lead.

And it's up to all in a society to understand it well.

Because followership also is a powerful force. It is trust. It is empowerment. It is future-making. Trust, empower, and make leaders out of those whose visions you wish to see imparted on the world. Who harbor in them something cosmic and worth following. Don't seek to lead. Seek justice, honesty, and harmony. Seek life, purpose, and spirit. And in so seeking, lead only when you must, follow only when you should.

~

Activism

Seek to understand before you speak. If it takes years to understand, take years to speak. Listen before you act. When it comes time to act, organize strong leadership to do so. Because from leaders are born communities. From communities, the tidal wave of change. And the waves of change are often a new chorus introduced to an old song, to revelers too lost to hear the dissonance in their notes.

If the change cannot wait, empower the people that can lead well. If you are called to lead, lead well, and empower your followers to bring harmony.

Without good leadership, there is only dissonance. Don't let your voice fall into the fray. Don't be stubborn, when a different song is needed. Don't abandon your leader, simply because the song is slow. Time is not truth. Life is. So, find the right song. Find your part in the harmony. And secure the leadership needed to sweeten the voices and build the wave.

3.
Relationship

*

There is a simple, forever truth that emerged with the cosmos. A truth that winds through each being, and binds each being to every other. That is the truth of relationship. You are in relationship with each and every being, and each and every being is in relationship with you. The question is the form the relationship takes, and the degree of proximity.

In your self-relationship, be as you were born to be; earth made you whole, in the way it needed you. The way you were made plays a larger role that should not be disturbed. Cultivate and nourish yourself—so that you can do the same in the world. Don't allow a wayward society to twist you into an unnatural form. Remember your body, your soul, and your spirit are one. Be integrated, always.

In your familial relationships—chosen or given—be respectful, and forgiving. Honor elders, always. Nurture the young and provide the structure, guidance, and discipline they need. But don't underestimate either. With the earth, honor her cycles, and be within them.

In your partnerships, be honest. With your partners, be full. Whether you are one of the few with an expansive heart, gifted the care to bind with many, or you bear a focused, all-consuming heart, that finds in one person the power of resonance, remember to give each partnership its due.

Relationships are not the same as love. There are no forms in love—only love. Love is a force, of its own right. The relationship is a home. A duty and a gift. It is a shared space—uncared for, it becomes dilapidated, depressing. Tended to, it invigorates and enlivens. A home can be refurbished or expanded, with old halls given new character. It can be found or built or shared in many places. Relationship is your tether to others, to spirit, to life.

With each of these, remember: The plant that must be nurtured, cared for, watered, is the relationship, not the love. Love is the soil. Pleasure is the water. Communication is the light.

Find the harmony in these.

Ecology: the first relationship

What the Bantu and Khoisan knew, is what the Algonquin and Lakota knew across the Atlantic; and what the Aboriginal Peoples knew across the eastern seas. What is still known today. That all people come from the Earth, are nourished by the earth, and return to the earth. It's easily seen in the rise of life on the planet, and in its subsequent evolution. In the reliance of all this life on the perfect boons of great-grandmother earth.

No matter how much is discovered, or how far away you go, earth will always be your first home, your first caretaker, your first relationship. You have earth in your bones.

The rush of the river, the rustle of the leaves, the lull of the waves—each of these is calming because it sings to the spirit. The morning dew and the evening breeze soothe because they were once the sheltering embrace of your body, and will one day be again. *Mfinda*, the forest, is the space between worlds, between spirit and dust. *Nzadi*, the river, is the bridge between what was and what is. From the plant life and memory churning in its oceans and sleeping in its sediment, to the spirits and breezes sprinting through its forests and riding on its rivers, earth is your greatest living ancestor. Your first wise relative. Your perfect haven in the vastness of the cosmos.

This relationship, between you and her and all her children, is ancient and enduring. It enriches and fulfills. It keeps safe and nourishes completely. And all its beneficiaries are called to honor it. To honor the gifts the earth has always given, and to assume the responsibility of care, respect, and keeping.

The earth gives air to breathe, soil to feed, fruit and fish and fowl to eat. The earth led us to cattle, and clay, and healing herbs. The earth gives us each fiber of skin, trickle of blood, strand of hair. Even when betrayed, the earth cleans up the messes left by some of its inhabitants. She sucks pollutants from the air, and cleans them from the water. Always, she gives. Always, she endures. Any child of hers that harms her, hurts itself and all her children ten times more. Don't make the earth choose between children.

People should not try to replicate what the earth gives—because what the earth gives is living, and what is done artificially, mechanically, never lives. People should never mechanize earth's systems, nor should they attempt to replace them. As with family, nothing should be done without love.

To live in harmony with the earth, is to understand her. To heed her wise counsel. To follow as she leads, and to pass down this knowledge. The earth imparts much when you listen, and gives much when you honor her.

This is why the greatest temples are with the trees, and by the sea. Why the earth herself is a place of reverence. Earth is not a thing to be conquered or tricked or used. Earth is a being to be lived with. Nature is not a place to be trekked into—nature is someone to be. Someone who lives inside and around you, who has been stolen from, disrespected, and threatened too often. Destroying life, to build on top of it, is a great evil. Build in and with life instead.

The earth is not yours because you own it. The earth is yours because you are it. Earth is the web in which each of us is a thread. The relationships between you and the earth and all things is sacred. To do right by it is simple: Honor the cycles of the earth and be within them. Don't force the earth to be useful; understand what she already gives and nurture it. Do always that which is regenerative, and that which moves as the earth does, feels as the earth feels. Avoid that which depletes. Avoid that which replaces the relationship between earth and earth-child. Choose leaders who will honor the relationship. Trust those who have honored it longest; reject those who have led its destruction and now claim to have answers.

Remember: earth is the relative who has always loved you.

~

Tending

Tending is a sacred endeavor. We are at our fullest when we tend to gardens, to the earth, and to each other. We are wise when we tend to ourselves.

~

Devotion

Of all love, of all honor, devotion is the deepest manifestation. Devotion is patient, it does not rush. Devotion is honest, and true to life. Devotion is a deep well. In it can be found peace, comfort, nourishment.

A key to living is understanding that which is worth being devoted to. The way of these pages. Life, spirit, and the cosmos. All that which nourishes and inspires, and all that which is asked of you by those worthy of asking. Those you love who love you back, and those who bring you closer to the world of spirit, the promise of life, and the truth of you.

Be devoted to life, and to the song of the spirit. Be devoted to who you could be, to justice, and earth. Be devoted to gratitude, to honesty, and to depth. Because these are courageous things.

Devotion is a power, and devotion is a gift. So don't misuse that power by devoting yourself to things that aren't right. Don't abuse that gift by giving it to someone who wouldn't live by these truths.

Be discerning, always, in your devotion. But once given, give it fully and without relenting. Give it as best you can, and then give it better.

Return to the well, often. Bring only those you trust.

Love

Love is the birthplace of life. It is the force that grows in the gaps between resonant notes, the overtone that swells and consumes them. Love is a new home.

The first love is cosmic. It is alive. Extant and conferred. Never beginning and never yielding. The next love is familiar. Found at birth, and rediscovered in people through life. The greatest love—true, raw, deep, high romantic love—is communal. Born in the resonance of spirit.

Each of these forms is, at its core, the same. It is the all-love. And the all-love is cosmic, familiar, and communal.

Be discerning in your devotion, but generous in your love.

Because love is communion, not contract. It does not mandate by time, by intensity, or by rules. It is simply borne. It is simply shared.

How people structure their lives in love is theirs to explore. Theirs to understand, and come to know, and adapt. The meaning of rules, structure, and commitment—these are terms of art in the practice of a love. And each love is practice. It's a daily devotion. A service. A bond and a being that must be kept, and a part of the great cosmic love that imbues all things.

Without love, there is no life. Without love, there is suffering.

This is why love should be central to every society, to every family, and to every person.

Always remember the love of the earth. Remember the love of the spirit, and the love of the cosmos. Allow it to fill you, whenever you can. Allow it to fill you, when you find love in others. Allow it to fill you, when you find love in a moment. Wherever there is truth and honor and justice—look to see if there is also love, and you will find it.

Love is what makes the heavy, light. Love is what binds in truth, and bears witness in darkness. Love is the first principle of true justice. The only path to joy, and health, and harmony. Shared and acknowledged, love becomes the greatest home for intimacy.

82

Do not seek love. Be in love, always.
Discover and rediscover love. Know love, and
give love. Because love is what the spirit
knows. When the spirit speaks, listen. And you
will be heard.

The greatest journey

The greatest journey is not the journey inwards, but the journey outwards. To look out is to understand what is within. It's to see how the fabric of all things weaves you, and how the truth of all things empowers you. It's to see that the dust of the stars is the same as the dust of your bones. That the waters of the earth are the blood of your veins. That the same mountain that burned what once was, is the mountain that erupts you into being.

To understand what is within you is to understand the cosmos. To heed the song of spirit is to commune with the worlds it births. It is to be alive and with god.

When you journey, be insular in your reflection, or whenever you must be. Be communal in your reverence, whenever you can be. Don't be deceived by those who cling stubbornly to self-righteousness or to the ways that led to injustice. When you find those who would follow the way of life, be with them. Where you find those who would not, avoid them. Because some diseases confuse the mind and spirit, before they do the body. But the truth is always the truth.

As in all things, remember the cycle. Remember it is constant. Remember each stage of the cycle is itself a cycle. And know that each stage varies in length.

Know your journey will move in this cycle, and know it is, itself, a part of it. Wherever you go, look around you—there are little answers everywhere. Whatever you think, think bigger—there are greater truths in the depths of every thought.

Allow yourself to be fully alive, and immerse yourself in the song of the spirit. Then, you will discover your deepest truths.

~

4.
Being well

✳

To be well is to be rooted. In the truth of
the cosmos and of all that you are. In the truth
of all there is, and all that *it* is. To be rooted in
reverence, and life, and spirit.

This kind of wellbeing requires many
things. It means tending to your body, your
mind, and your spirit. It means tending to your
relationships—past, present, future, eternal. It
means tending to the world around you
through your work, words, and actions.

It is returning your thoughts, always, to an
honest understanding of the way things are,
and the way they are meant to be. And it is
creating space to be more as you can be—the
daily, lifelong practice of living up to your
promise.

Being well is not only an act of care, but a
practice of cultivation. It is nurture, and it is

discipline. It is change, and it is flow. To be well is to be right with all things.

So, tend to your health not because it's advantageous to you—but because life is as much a duty as it is a gift. If you are unhealthy, you can't live up to your promise or achieve yourself at your truest and highest. And if you can't become that great you, if you can't begin to make history—both personal and collective history—then, in truth, you were never really here. And the world suffered for it.

There is the knowing about living deeply, and then there is living deeply. Tend to your health as you would tend to what matters most. Because it is the first step in the *practice* of living deeply.

~

Body

The body, like the earth, is sacred. It's your piece of the planet. A pebble in the sea that lines the coast.

If you would avoid polluting the earth, avoid polluting the body. The body is the earth, and it does for you what the earth does. It gives as the earth gives, and receives the boons the earth grants. Just as the moon tugs on the tides, it beats in the blood. Just as the daylight dances in the forest, it swells in your heart. Given the choice and the power:

Would you cut down the forest?

Would you send smoke into the air, pour poison in the sea?

Would you pile trash onto the land?

If not, then don't send smoke into your lungs, or poison into your blood. Don't fill yourself with trash or allow your health to fail. Avoid drugs that shorten life, threaten health, or alter your body's nature.

Devote yourself, instead, to partaking in the bounty the earth has given. Eat mindfully, and with respect. Indulge only in what the earth gives, and avoid the imitations and derivatives that would pollute you as they pollute the world you live in. Move your body, as the earth moves. Cherish the organic.

Remember that the body is a sacred domain. What is within its world is yours, just as what is in the earth is hers. A body's organs, tissues, and parts should not be separated from it, except in the natural way. Even the living body of another, growing in the womb, is a visitor in a large place. Until it passes from the cradle of the body to the cradle of the day, it holds no agency above its bearer.

Don't allow your mind to convince you that your body is wrong. Don't allow the failings of a society to create within you a dislike for yourself. Understand beauty is not what your mind decides, or simply what a society decides—it is cosmic, and it is as clear as water. Bodies are born with beauty. The task is to keep them so, and to grow them so. Fit and healthy and balanced, honored with exercise and rest and clean nourishment. Mind your body, because it is all bodies. It is the earth, it is the cosmos, and it is a gift.

Keep your body fit, and your mind healthy. Sleep. Breathe clean air. Wash your hands *well* and often. Tidy your surroundings. Eat real, whole food. Wear clean, organic fabrics. Let yourself discover and allow yourself pleasure. These simple things are what keep the body vibrant. And in the vibrant body, the spirit can flourish.

~

Spirit

Keep yourself healthy.
Love and live with courage.
Transform.
Understand what it is to be rooted,
and be so.
Return to center.
Do not wait to live.

~

Mind

Remember the mind is a place. You have to care for it, as with any other place that is part of your home.

Nurture it, with calm and sleep. Pleasure it, with intimacy and entertainment. Nourish it, with good knowledge and good food.

Don't pollute the mind, because a polluted thing grows untethered from the truth of the cosmos. Avoid drugs that warp the mind, change its nature, or cheapen pleasure.

Give your mind, instead, the gifts of music and mystery. Let your mind off its leash— allow yourself to dream and give your mind the space to wander. Create and move like water. Think deeply, at times, and at other times, not at all. Allow yourself leisure and find the truth in laughter. Often.

This is what it means to keep that place clean.

Sometimes, the mind grows anxious. When this happens, don't force it to be different. Instead, soothe it with the truth of the cosmos. Remember all that is large, and how small the place on the earth in the galaxy in which you stand is. How small you are. Then, let go of awareness, and focus only on the feeling of your toes. And then your feet. And then your legs. And so on. Come back to the body slowly.

Sometimes, the mind grows heavy, or gray. When this happens, allow yourself grief. Often, this is weight upon the spirit. But within the week, immerse yourself in those gifts of music and mystery. Abandon leisure and embrace creation. Find company in those who would hold you up, and if you are alone here, remember you are never alone. Find comfort in the cosmic life all around you, even if you cannot hear it. Know it is there and know it embraces you. Find comfort in where you still could go, and how you still can transform. Find comfort in the truth: that your purpose is to live, and that's why you are here. Especially when it's difficult.

~

Family

Family is a gift that cannot be returned. No matter how poorly it may suit you. You are born into your family like you're born into your bones.

This is the first pillar to making sense of family: acknowledgment. Acknowledge that who you share blood with will always be who you share blood with.

But shared blood does not define your moments. You can be more transparent with some in your family and less with others. You might reveal some truths with everyone, but other truths with no one. You may find trust and joy in all members of your family, but at different times and in different ways.

But where there is trust or joy, let there also be love. Where there is love, let there be some trust, and some joy. Be quick to forgive, and slow to admonish. Be understanding, and be compassionate. Know each member, and what they understand, fear, and love. Respect these, and be with them through it. Listen before you speak.

Where there is not yet joy, or trust has been broken, remember: family living and past, is the forever knot in which you are tied. Like the body and mind, it tethers you elsewhere. With family, seek always to remedy what is broken—especially when it's difficult. If it will need time, let that time pass. If you cannot forgive, be sure you understand why. Because the burden will carry on long after you.

This is the second pillar of familial health: devotion. Don't decide it's impossible to mend a wound. Discover it's impossible. By trying. Where there is love and trust, be devoted to upholding it. Where there isn't, be devoted to restoring it. Where it cannot be restored, be devoted to healing from it.

Because it is in healing that truth is evident. All of humanity is one large, extended family. If you cannot heal wounds in your immediate family, how can you heal wounds in your extended? And if you cannot heal wounds in your extended, how can your mind and body ever be free, your spirit unburdened?

And if your mind, body, and spirit are always burdened, how can you truly live?

When the gift you are given is completely broken, and cannot be mended, one step remains. Gift yourself anew. Discover, in the world, a different family. One where love and trust can flourish. If it can't be discovered, create it. In even one other person, truly loved and cherished, family can be rediscovered. In even one other person, truly trusted, familial health can be restored. In even one other person, worth devoting to, what seems impossible becomes real.

And even having found yourself in a family, with love and trust, you can find a second family. Create a third. Each family can grow.

Because a healthy family is a gift. You can receive it, and you can give it. And you're not limited to one.

~

Society

What proceeds is a version of a story told many times before, by teachers in many topics.

Imagine one day, you are walking through the forest.

As you walk, you turn and come across a clearing. There, you see a bird has died and lies quietly on the grass.

You may wonder, "what went wrong for the bird," and move on.

Now imagine again, you are walking through the same forest. You walk, you turn, and you come across the same clearing. Only this time, you see hundreds of birds, of all kinds, lying silent, dead. And the grass here looks dead too. Even as you stand at the edge, a bird flies from the forest over the clearing, and it suddenly falls, dead, to the ground.

You could ask, "what is wrong with the birds?"

But you would be right to ask, "what is wrong with this clearing," and head back towards the safety of the forest.

The first response, focused only on the birds, is how society sometimes treats its members.

A society's leaders and influencers will see that problems are arising—in the health of people's bodies, or with the health of their minds. The society will ask, "what is causing this epidemic?" And it will ask, "what is wrong with these people?"

But rarely will it ask what it should really be asking, which is, "what is wrong with our society?" Because too often, people are told to fix themselves, when it's the society that is broken. Begin, always, with the society.

With an unhealthy society, you can train your body and still find disease. With an unhealthy society, you can nourish your mind and still find it unstable. An unhealthy society may not even know it is unhealthy.

With deep-enough brokenness, the public of an unhealthy society will learn to believe that those having a healthy response to an unhealthy situation are the ones with the problem. They will search for medicines and therapies and ideas to try and fix them. The hope is that these people will be able, again, to function in the system in which the society is embedded. To relearn the lies that broke it. And to return to the approach they are used to.

When it's these same systems, teachings, and approaches that led the society to ruin.

Sometimes, when enough things are going wrong, it's time to stop looking at individuals and start examining a society. Sure, some problems really are specific. And yes, each person must be responsible for keeping themselves healthy. Each person must tend to themselves, to truly live.

To do so means to care for the mind, and to care for the body, and to care for the spirit.

But it also means to care for the society. Because in this life, the mind exists in the body. Together, they ground the spirit. But the body and mind exist in the society. And to be tethered to a broken society is to weigh on the spirit. And that is a collective brokenness. The world deserves better. You deserve better.

Make better. Be active in choosing leaders, and follow only those blessed with good leadership. Allow yourself to be insular when you must. Have the courage to abandon a society when it will not change, and to help create what could be when you believe it can. Understand first, what could be, and learn, always, all that it entails. Strive to create health. Strive to create a place where healthy minds and bodies can flourish. Where spirits can be unburdened, and where life can thrive. Tend what is around you as you would tend to yourself. Until both are whole.

This is what it means to have a healthy society.

~

Wealth

True wealth is in the world we are born into. The earth's desecration, its sequestration, its abuse, are what limit the access of all to this abundant birthright.

True wealth is in the harmonic flow of things. In abundant health, boons, and ability. True wealth is the reverberation, the reflection, of realized potential. Wealth is the overflowing life.

Wealth should grow based on what is given, not taken.

Creation is the greatest gift. Peace is another. True justice, health, and wellbeing still others.

And there are the gifts of knowledge, and cultivation, and change. Wisdom and joy and beauty. Nourishment, care, and leadership.

True wealth is not an empty accumulation. True wealth is a greater recognition. It is an empowerment, and a gift by those well-served. The more profoundly each is served, the more they should gift. The purpose of wealth isn't to be wealthy. It's to find liberty.

Do not seek wealth for wealth's sake. Seek liberation for living's sake.

Too often, wealth breeds resentment, frustration, or jealousy. These are misplaced. What's wrong in a society is not when there is wealth; wealth is good and natural. What is wrong is when wealth is the precursor to basic wellbeing—a situation which is unnatural. All people, born into this world, are given the gift of life. And this gift should be cherished, and cultivated, not only by each person, but by the society. Wealth should be the response, and never the call.

What can be wrong, also, is the way in which wealth is achieved. True wealth is born of vision, good leadership, and cultivation. True wealth is born of harmony, creation, and service. What is born of violence, artificial extraction, or undue inheritance is not wealth, but disease. The creation of this kind of wealth can only be balanced by its usage—when it's used to repair, create, and protect harmony, justice, and beauty in the world.

The greatest wealth, the largest cluster of abundance in a place, is always communal—because it is always the fruit of the earth. When one rises a lot, all should rise a little. When one falls a lot, all should fall a little. Reject societies that would kill—people, the earth—to extract more wealth. Embrace, instead, what gives, and what enlivens.

~

Ownership

What can ever be owned, but that which is freely given? Was not the land given to all of us? Are we not given to the land? The earth does not belong to you, you belong to it. The earth is not a thing to own, it is a living ancestor to honor. The earth gifts you its body to make a home. This home is yours. The earth made you siblings to trade with. What is traded is yours. What is gifted is yours. What is agreed upon is yours. But don't confuse trade, gifts, and agreements with extraction, conquest, and theft. The first are based in life. The latter in violence. True ownership is a living practice. A responsibility. Steward it well.

~

5.

Making sense of yourself

✳

The truth of who you are is both the eternity of who you've been and the reality of who you're becoming. It's not enough to say, "this is who I am." If you really want to make sense of yourself, you should ask, "who can I be? Who should I be? How?"

It's also not enough to say, "this is what I want." To make sense of yourself, you need to consider what others, what the collective spirit, and what a world bursting to change might need from you.

Doing this isn't always easy. Sometimes, it requires a reframing of how you think about yourself, your many identities, and how you relate to others. It requires overcoming certain assumptions or popular ideas, and sometimes, it requires a bit of loneliness—or at least, the courage to stand alone. It requires escaping the shallow, and the stagnant, and allowing yourself to go deeper. To be honest. To transform and be reborn into who you can and should be. Into whom, at your highest, you were born to be.

Because what is true, is that who you can and should be is, in part, hinted from the moment of your birth. The realities of your body, mind, and spirit in that moment of first light are not only questions of what society sees in you, but rather, truths of the vessel the cosmos have called down as an agent, in this form, for this lifetime. They reflect a promise of what you can do for others and who you can become. A reminder that your body is the vibrant earth, and that you are the spark and the void and the living sun. They are not a limitation, but a question:

Will you rise?

To return to center is to begin to answer that question. To understand its meaning, its power, and its promise. To understand its nuances and pitfalls. Understanding this is what it means to make sense of yourself.

~

Identity

At times, so much is made of an identity that it leaves people living in an illusory world. As one moves through life, it's easy to believe that a society is the world, or that this reality is the whole cosmos. But that is a mistake.

Your time here is one part of a great cosmic cycle. It is a stop in the journey of your soul, and it is the day of your spirit. Do not waste it trying to uncover or recreate a list of things to be. Especially not when they are derived from categories, language, and assumptions created within a society.

Because to do so is to erect a wall between yourself and the earth. It's to become lost in the folds of a society, and deaf to the expanse of the spirit. It's to ignore the bright power of the cosmos around and within you, and to die, instead, a little death. It is to kill something beautiful that, like god, does not ask to be named, or categorized, or branded but simply *is*. Learn to recognize when you are doing this, and when those around you are doing it. And abandon it.

If you have come to do it over many years, or if it has come to bring you comfort, reconsider it. Do not confuse the resounding power of the history inside you with the trends of the world around you. Avoid the lie that says that what is broken is you, when what is broken is your society. Understand that the discomfort you may feel, the feeling you want to escape the bones the earth gave you, the feeling that you are being seen in a false way, is a feeling. And what it is telling you may not be what a society has taught you to hear.

Understand too, when the mind is ill, or when the spirit is weighty, from where that illness and weight originate. Because the mind does not become ill of its own accord; it becomes infected by the burdens of trauma, inherited or encountered. The experience is the symptom, and not the source. It's the symptom of a body and mind overwhelmed, and, often, a symptom of a place broken.

So, understand when it is the society you look to escape, and not the bones. Understand that to be a full and living being is not to transcend, but to delve.

Remember: every shape you've ever taken is exactly that—a shape. So don't let it stop your flow. Don't allow the failures of a society to convince you to adopt within yourself an attachment to certain words. Don't allow the desire to feel different, or the honest feeling that you *are* different from others in a society, to convince you that you need a new way of being seen. Because more often, it is the society that needs changing.

You are already unique. There is no need to find comfort in problems, or community in categories. There is no need to create new names for old realities, or to make reasons for why there may be pain in your heart just so that others can understand it. They don't need to. There's already someone who understands. There is already cosmic love that is with you, always. And the truth of this, the truth of all things, already lives within you.

There is a need, instead, to discover the spirit. To be silent. And to be full. To live in purpose and delve into the life you were given. To understand the history in which you are embedded, and the future in which you will be immersed. To unburden yourself from learned obsessions, shared assumptions, and social distractions. Because a person cannot just "be themselves" in a society that is not itself. A living thing cannot thrive in a place that has lost its tether to life.

So let pain be pain. Its true resolution doesn't come from escape, or new attitudes, self-discovery or any single identity. Its true resolution comes from living, until you are called to live no more. It comes from changing what's around you, not just what's inside you. And it comes from cultivating the health of the mind, the body, and the spirit.

It comes from creating a healthy society and discovering yourself anew in the song of the spirit. It comes from being rooted in what's much larger, and what's much deeper. Always return to it.

~

Mastery

When, in the same lifetime, you have lived and died many times over—begun and ended and begun again. When you have nurtured the mind and cultivated the body. When you stand high in the sky, after years of slowly rising. Then you have mastery.

Mastery is a state in which you live—not a one-time achievement. It's an important point in any cycle of growth, whether it be general, or whether it relates to a specific craft, artform, or practice. To achieve mastery is to reach high noon, to shine your brightest, and to be your warmest. It's to be greatly skilled (not just talented) at something. It's to live wisely and fulfilled. It's to be assured. Mastery is the strength of your being, realized.

It takes, at minimum, years. It can take a lifetime. Even once reached, there is more mastery to be stepped into.

This is why it's important to understand, about cultivation, that it never truly ends. It is a cycle of waxing and waning, slowly larger, until the brightness is total. It is a moment of standing high in the sky before a setting and then rising again.

~

Personal experience

When you realize the effects of a society on your personal experience, that's only the first step. When you realize its effects on everyone's experience, you have understood something much more powerful. Don't get watered down by your own experience. Don't confuse perspective for truth, and don't confuse study and training for knowledge. Truth is deeper than both. Understand the cosmic experience in which you're a part. Then, understand your role in it.

~

Courage

To do these things, many of them, requires profound courage. To live fully requires the same. Courage is the energy that overcomes fear. While some courage burns in the hearth of the heart, the spirit contains limitless courage, because it is fearless. When your mind is without courage, or your body will not move, remember your spirit. Forget your position, and be guided, instead by what lies beneath. Be guided by that deepest truth that has always been you.

Because your spirit is a link to all that was and is and will be. Your spirit is the thing that hurts in life, and finds peace after. Your spirit is what truly loves, and what glows in any darkness. Your spirit can speak to those who once were, and those who will be. It's not a possession, but a being. Your spirit is you.

Let your spirit show you the courage to live. Then, be courageous in living. Let your spirit guide your courage to love. And be courageous in that love. Let the spirit find you courage to understand your promise, and then embrace and pursue that promise. The spirit knows what the body can't yet know. It hears what is silent, and sees before the eyes or even the mind do. It is the you that bears the here, the there, and the always.

Don't defer to others to live. Don't look for permission or acceptance to take the rooted path. Seek only courage. Find that courage in the call of the wind and the warmth of the sun. Find that courage by the light of the moon, and the rush of the waves. Find that courage by the heavy peace of the forest, or in a quiet room, with fragrant incense.

Find that courage in these pages, and in the song of the spirit.

Transformation

Transformation is what you do when there is nothing else to be done—or when there is everything still to be done. When one part of the cycle, fulfilled, is ready to birth another. Transformation is a resounding culmination of all that a being has become, and a return to it. It is a beginning anew, and a becoming again.

Too often, people are afraid of change. But there is god in change. Change is the fire of life. At every threshold, from the time before birth, to the time of it, to the time that follows. In every moment within a moment. In the crossing from this world to the first world. In your experience of these events, and in the experience of those who witness. Change is baked into the skin of reality. It colors everything. To resist it, is to resist life itself.

Rather than looking to stop change, seek to affect its course. Transform always in the direction of life, and in the direction of the spirit. Grow always deeper, and not shallower.

Be more honest, especially when doing so takes courage. Be nurturing, and not abrasive, in transforming reality. Transformation isn't found in what you ingest, or in what you inhale—what's altered through consumption is only perception, and perception is illusory. Transformation is found far past perception, in the depths of the spirit and in immersing in life.

Cultivate in yourself a harbor for transformation. Cultivate it in your home, your community, and your society. Don't always try or push or force. Be guided, always, by the song of the spirit. Allow the spirit to guide transformation, and when you cannot see, listen. When you cannot listen, be.

If you live in a place that is not guided in such a way, refuse to be swayed. When you are surrounded by people who are not inspired by the song of the spirit, pay them no mind. Transform yourself not for them, but for life, for the earth that bears you, and for all that holds you up. Live in the way that's rooted, and answer the call of the cosmos.

Transformation is the path by which we move through the cycles of life. It's the path of the earth, and the cosmos, and your ancestors. It's the path of your spirit, and the path of your mind. As with the cosmos, and the earth, make sure that each transformation is more beautiful than the last. Don't allow the cruelties of a society to transform you. Don't allow the injustices others impart to guide your transformation. And don't allow violence to transform your society into something ugly.

Embrace the life that bubbles within you. Those echoes of always—and the promise of forever. Each seed of change is a gift of life. Live, and be transformed.

~

Rebirth

Each day you are born again. Like the sun and the earth's movements around it. Like the petals and the leaves that furl and unfurl. Like the steady hum of life in all things.

If you feel wrong one day, be different the next. Sleeping and waking are part of a daily cycle of living and dying. They allow you to escape, to learn, and to grow. And this means you are never stuck. Because each day is a new life.

~

6.

The nature of wrongness

❋

A wrong is the stain that can't be escaped.
There are noble wrongs, of course. But the
deepest wrongs never are. They are the ones
that ignore the truth of the cosmos. The
violent assault on the cycles of nature. The
habit of accepting social norms as they
become acceptable, but rejecting natural
norms when they have always been true. The
mistake of assuming who you are, or what the
world is, when you have not yet really begun
to shape either.

Wrongness is not an identity, but a state of
being. It is not some evil thing that requires
battle, but a disease that requires healing.
Something that, left unchecked, can envelop,
or drown. Something that, unhealed, festers
and spreads. But the thing about a state of
being is, it can always be shed. And to shed
that state of being requires a few things.

Before anything else, comes acknowledgment. An understanding of what went wrong, that it was indeed wrong, and that it needs mending.

The next three are cosmic truths, required of and real for all things in life, and everything that matters.

First, is knowledge. To *only* acknowledge and then act might make it worse. Take the time to learn about wrongness, and also to learn about healing. Be humble, and curious, and engaged.

Next, is devotion. Devote yourself to addressing and redressing the wrongness until it has been made right.

Finally, comes practice. Wrongness is not something that a single action will bind or heal, but something that requires consistent, unyielding practice to make right.

~

The uncentered life

The uncentered life is an odyssey of loss. It is missed opportunity, for actualization but also for making the world better. It is a lifetime of grief and disconnect. It is a rooting in all that is wrong, and an uprooting from all that is true.

It is what happens when people seek to understand what and how, but not why. It is what happens when people accept the living lie that life, living, the spirit are not worthy of reverence. When a society treats the natural cycles of the body, the mind, the earth as inconveniences to be dominated, rather than what they are: sacred truths to be learned from.

This first wrong stems not from malice, but from ignorance. From not knowing. And then from not committing. And then from not doing.

So, know. Devote. Do. Be rooted in the truth of the cosmos, of the spirit, and of nature. Live these truths because to do so is to find your way back to why you're here, and

who you are. To find a key to the world as it
should be and can be. So first become rooted,
and then grow into yourself, and into life, as
they are meant to be.

~

Violence

Violence is the intentional, avoidable, or reckless violation, harming, or injury of the body, and the havoc it wreaks on the mind and the weight it casts upon the spirit of the doer and the recipient.

It is not enough to avoid violence. One must do what they can to remove it from a community, and a society, entirely. And one must not use violence to do so. That is the challenge.

Empower communication, of the deepest kind. Through full communication, without barriers, and without room to escape or overpower, most conflicts can be understood.

Then, through the work of repair, through partnership and with time, most conflicts can be resolved.

Sometimes, violence is truly unavoidable. When it's the only way to protect yourself, or someone else. When it's the only way to prevent harm. Even then, be reluctant. Use that violence which does not maim. This is defense, not war. Because violence that kills or maims only wreaks havoc on the living cosmos, on the body, and on the society. So, be careful, always, with the bodies of others, and be careful, always, with your own.

Defense is the work of protection. Don't allow those in a society tasked with protecting or securing it to use violence against those they are meant to protect.

War—maximizing or planning violence on the imagined behalf of a society—is never justified. Fight no war but the war in these pages. Fight no war but the war of life.

The only natural violence is the kind needed to feed from another animal. As is the natural way, this should be done with respect, care, and while minimizing suffering. The rest is a mistake.

Because violence breeds tragedy. Violence is the antithesis of vibrance, and fullness, and health. Violence is a dissonant chord in the song of life. It is the thing that makes ugly. Accept it sparingly—in defense, and for life.

~

Deception

The worst kind of deception is self-deception. Don't deceive others. But more importantly and more forgotten, don't deceive yourself. Don't cheapen a powerful thing by making falsehoods of it, or yourself claim falsehoods, or amplify them. Because in this cheapening, honesty and justice are lost. Be honest. Vigorously. Relentlessly. And grow from it.

~

Technology and the artificial

No matter how complex its workings, no matter how awesome its outputs, the artificial never lives.

Technology, simply put, is the application of knowledge towards a purpose. This is, on its own, a fundamental part of existence. But as with lives lived, laws written, and systems entrenched—technologies can harm or heal. While in the short term, they may do both, at the scale of lifetimes, technologies eventually prove to be more destructive or more creative.

One of the easiest ways to distinguish which a technology will be—killer or healer— is the degree to which it is rooted in life. Does it follow the earth's cycles, or threaten them? Does it learn from and move with earth's billions of years of wisdom, or think itself wiser? Does it honor the sacred, or seek to replace what should never be replaced?

Marvels of mechanization should be grounded, always, in the rhythm of the cosmos. Where they attempt to replicate or mimic, they are wayward. Where they exist to dominate or destroy, they are lost. Where they replace or determine, they are not marvels at all, but curses.

Do not confuse the curse for the marvel.

Life isn't only physical, but spiritual. Each human being is a meeting of mind, body and spirit. To devalue this, to equate person to machine or machine to person, is the worst violence. When people refuse to hear the truth of the cosmos, or devalue what is sacred, they burden their own spirits with the weight of the mistake, and, in doing so, burden all.

So, value the person because the person shines. Value the organic, because the organic lives. Shun the artificial—because it does neither. Let tools be tools, and don't elevate their status. Use them for their ease—but reject tools with a propensity for destruction, or which disrupt the cycles of life or the earth, or that use you, rather than you them. Remember: you have choice. Become free from attachments to the artificial. Embrace what lives. Remember: truth is in the cosmos.

~

7.

Living in practice

✳

Life is practice. It's the million ways you came to be, and the billion more you are still becoming. It is the intermission of your spirit's sleep, and its journey in this realm. It is the responsibility you've been given, and how you observe it.

Life is service. It is everything you are called to be, and the core of who you can become. It's the little things, the everything, that you are meant to do.

Life is now. It is not tomorrow. It is not "what if?" It's what happens while you're wondering. It's what's already there when you are searching. It's what's already yours when you wish you had more.

A person, living well, can die at any time and be full. But that doesn't mean they should.

Death is good when it follows a long, healthy, and abundant life. When it does not hurt. When it is in the comfort and company of love.

Where there is violence, pain, or loneliness in a death—or when it interrupts—there is tragedy.

But tragedy does not negate life.

Remember always that to live is to move through cycles. It is to create the society where violence, pain, and loneliness have fewer and fewer places to roost. It is to understand you are a moment in the cosmos, and a dream of the earth. That you, like all living beings, are the agent through which the spirit acts.

Remember that the dead are to be revered, and the living honored. Remember that all that goes, lives in you for as long as you love it, cherish it, and honor it. No person, still loved, cherished, and honored, truly dies. No spirit remembered is without tether to this world. All that are loved are kept alive. All that live in memory live here.

To change, from body to spirit to living energy, is one rising and setting. And come morning, there is a rising again.

Honor those you love, for all your life. And they too, will live for all your life. Remember those you knew, and pass their memory forward through time. And they too, will live on through the years. With each generation that keeps them.

In this, find the truth. In your own spirit, find the never-ending continuity of all that is soulful. In your own body, find the rhythms and fullness of the earth. Your spirit bears the living waters to which all spirits, departed, return. Your body bears the elements to which all bodies, lifeless, come back. There is no end to those you love. And there is no end to you. There is only, always, change. Love this change because it loves you. Because it is the world and life themselves. Bear always witness to those you would want to see immortalized.

And long after they go, honor them in your conversations, dreams, and rituals. Long after they are ancestors, sit with them, and commune with them, and they will be with you—even as they could never be in life. And should the day come that no one is alive to remember them—when, formless, they adjoin with the light of the cosmic sea, become a voice in the chorus of spirits heard only in prayer—still they will be felt. In the forest, in the wind between the trees. By the lake, in the calm of trickling ripples. In the room with burning incense, where someone, a great descendant in deep reverence and contemplation, reflects on the song of the spirit.

So, pass this knowledge forward, too. And never forget:

Life is the pregnant, eternal moment.

It is forever and it is always and it is you.

Do not wait to live.

~

Art

Art is the work of bringing existence to life. It is the culmination, the exploration, the interpretation of experience. It is the connection between what is and what waits to burst through. It is the gift of every person, and the calling of a few. It grows. It transforms. It becomes.

Art is in the leaves and bark. Art is in your fingertips, and it clings to your pores. Art is the world as it is, has been, and could be.

Life is art.

~

Work

At its most basic, the work of any animal is to stay alive. To secure food, water, mates. But if you zoom out, you see what cosmic eyes see—when an animal does its work, it does the work of the ecosystem. In eating or not eating, hunting or not hunting, mating or not mating, it contributes to or detracts from the harmony of the world. As it works, it gives life to other things and it enables the larger system to breathe.

And this is the truth: we work for each other. We fulfill our roles so that others may fulfill theirs. This is why it's important to live in a society where role and purpose are explored and understood. Because a role isn't something to keep a machine running, or a broken reality afloat. It's a calling. And when a broken society conflates this calling with empty tasks or extractive violence, when it forces you to uphold its brokenness, it becomes difficult to hear the calling.

To work is to heed this calling, and to give your heart to it. To invest your being in it.

Your work should bring you sustenance, and it should also bring value to others. It should serve your purpose, and the world's wellbeing. And it should set you on the path to living up to your promise. The greatest work is the work of the song of spirit. Live it. Discover in it, somewhere, your promise. And remember; purpose, promise don't care what your field is—they demand to be lived in any field you find yourself in.

Don't confuse the power of the calling with what a society wants you to do. Don't abandon your life and spirit because of your need for sustenance, and don't deprive your life and spirit because you wouldn't work to sustain yourself. Keep with you the greater role of work in the harmony of things.

Work well, not just hard. Work well to be able to live well. Work well to be able to live out your promise. Hard work is worthy of respect, but alone, it's not something to strive for. Strive, instead, for *good* work. Because good work upholds life.

~

Study

Study as you would live; well, and fully. Embrace knowledge about the nature of things.

But remember always that the deepest knowledge is in the earth, and in the cosmos. It cannot be separated from the fullness in which it swims. The ocean spray is still the ocean. And the ocean is still the earth. And the earth is still the cosmos. And the cosmos is in you.

So, study first the song of the spirit. It is knowledge of the first kind. Study it, embrace it, more deeply than anything else. And discover in it the deep truths that books and separation, dissection and speculation, cannot teach.

Respect all that is sacred.

Don't confuse observation with understanding, or function with purpose.

See life for all it is. And avoid attempts to control it.

Live it instead.

~

Growth

As with all change, and all life, growth is a sum of cycles, itself a cycle, and part of cycles, all at once. It is a fluid motion from one state into the next. It is cultivated, with time, nourishment, and experience. At its truest, growth is living.

When you think of growth, understand it is not a thing that ends, but a truth that is. Growth is. It is the dance of life—its steps and starts and flourishes. Twirls and chants and stomps. Growth is the summoning, and truth the summoned.

Organic growth, of all kinds, tapers and plateaus and rises. Don't fear this, love this. Growth that does not taper or plateau, growth that does not cycle threatens life, and should be avoided. Dance instead, as it dances. Move as it moves. Cycle with it, and become as it summons you to be.

True growth emerges from harmony. From health and immersion. From delving in the deepest depths. From the call of the spirit. It's what comes of honest change. Be honest,

always, with the spirit, and growth will fulfill.
Live in truth and in depth, and you will find
them in all that you become.

~

Adornment

Adornment is making art of the body. It is to make of yourself a place where the spirit can sing.

The first adornment is naked. It is the act of tending. Of becoming clean when your body calls for it—and letting your body be when it doesn't. Of sculpting the form with good movement. Of right nourishment.

The second adornment is layered. It's to adorn yourself with the bounty of the earth, and surround yourself with the same. To cherish the organic and reject the artificial. Because the organic is life—it is health, it is wellbeing. It is the gift the earth has always given, and it is tethered to the world of spirit. And the artificial is untethered, unhealthy, and ugly to the spirit.

And this is the final adornment. A truth. Understanding that adornment is not only a thing of the body, but a gift to the spirit. So, take care in how you adorn yourself, because adornment is a bringing to life of all that you are, have been, and will be. It is a bringing to life of who you seek to become. It is an embodiment of the song of the spirit.

Wear it well.

~

8.

How to hear the spirit.

✳

In the quiet morning, wading through the mist of sleep-was-just-here. With the rich aroma of incense, that still carries in it a part of the forest. Naked—in body and spirit—in the hypnotic warmth of a shower or bath. In fasting, prayer, and creation. In communion.

At moonrise, too, outside and by the fire. With the beat of a drum, deep, steady, in your chest. In the wild dance of the night, and the embodiment of all that you are, all that you bear, and all you desire.

In the little moments of epiphany hidden between the pages of this book. In the call of the heart, heard in someone else, found while living in truth. In the blissful rest of service to those who deserve it.

In the eternity of the sea, as you stand watching, listening, feeling on the coast. In the depths of the forest with the old trees. In the fullness of the heart, with an elder, or child, you love.

In all these places, the spirit lives loudest. In all these places, the spirit shines, the spirit breathes, the spirit possesses. When you cannot hear it, seek it here. Embrace these, and it will make itself known to you. Unmissable.

~

Quiet

To make quiet, in the early morning, is to make space for the spirit. It is to create a place within yourself to hear the call of ancestors, rippling in the waves of the living, eternal, cosmic ocean. It is to linger with the spirit, and to wait to return to the body.

It is to be weightless.

Quiet is as physical as it is existential. It's in the act of creating cleanliness in your mouth when you brush after waking. It's in creating space within your body with a small fast to allow your bowels to move. And of course, it's creating space within your mind and heart by waiting a while before you speak or work or turn to distracting stimulus.

Quiet is avoidance of noise of all kinds. From the noise of a broken society to the noise of a shallow way of living. Quiet is also an opportunity to delve into the song of the spirit. To spend time in communion, creation, reflection. In truth and resonance.

~

Communion

If you have found in your life, that you have prayed, and gone unanswered, one of three things will be true.

First: that you have misunderstood the purpose of prayer. Prayer is not to ask and receive. Prayer is not to manifest. Prayer is not extraction. Like all true relationships, prayer is communion. It is conversation.

If you demand, but do not listen, you will not hear. If you desire, but do not serve, you will not receive. If you want, but do not live, you will not find.

Second: that you have not prayed, but thought. Don't pray with just the mind, or only with the body. Pray also with the spirit. The spirit can't be known through thought alone. The spirit can't be heard without space to speak. Live by the song, and the spirit will make itself known. Be comfortable, when you pray. Be quiet. Be spacious and clear. Let all your will sing with prayer—and you will be in conversation. And this form of conversation, this kind of connection—is *communion*. Which leads to the third possibility:

That you have not understood the nature of communion. Communion is the deepest form of connection, a tying and retying of spiritual knots. It is not a beseeching nor is it a begging. It is not only a matter of trust. It is a matter of truth.

God may be known by any of the many names god is given, but god transcends names, and place, and time, and people. God is not involved, and god does not work. God is, in all ways. Already there, always moving, and too great to move. God is not for seeking— god is for witnessing. Communion is for that next layer—the layer of layer of branching cosmos. Personal and collective, singular and plural, communion is for the spirit. For what listens and moves and involves and meddles. Because change and flow and life—these lives here and beyond—they are interwoven with the world of spirit. And the world of spirit works through the world of the living.

If you live by the song of the spirit, if you follow the rooted way of life, then the cosmic spirit, collective and ancient, manifold and one, will find in you a conduit. And in life's great tapestry, the world will open for you to unfold into your purpose and your promise.

Prayer is for conversation. For company and for comfort. *Life* is where the answers happen. Where the words of the spirit become the truth of the body—and the truth in the world.

Communion is for living. Focus on it. And see how it roots you. See how life answers.

~

Creation

In the fashion of all that came before you, in the tradition of great-grandmother earth, you were given the gift of creation. It is inherited. Generations old, and generations lived. The power of the cosmos to create lives within the fabric of your flesh. It dances in the daydreams that wander into your mind. Fills the seeds of life your body may harbor.

The act of creation is, itself, divine. It is a microcosm of the cosmic play.

When you create, you are a star, a planet, an ocean. You are the mountain erupting, the earth birthing, the skies pouring. When you create, you become something more, and you become more yourself. This is true of art, and childbearing, and gardening. Of crafting or cooking. Shaping or nurturing. Designing. Writing. All of it. It is the truth of things.

Create then, as you live. When done well, you will hear in it the song of the cosmos. You will see in it the truth of your spirit. That is beauty.

~

Silence

Sometimes, silence is needed more than quiet. Silence is void. The place from which life emerges. A sea with hidden depths. Where you go deeply, you discover it is vast, but rarely empty.

Because within its depths, brims life. A teeming, truthful life, thriving in its quiet haven. A haven that nurtures. Where peace is discovered, and the spirit can sing.

Find silence not only for the ears, but for the mind and eyes. Just as life takes after the place in which it exists, so do your body and mind. You become as your surroundings. In noisy surroundings, you too become noisy. Conflicted and confused. Concerned about everything and sometimes nothing at all. You feel a constant distraction, fog, anxiousness. In true silence, you can find peace.

It's this peace which gifts. This peace which holds fast and invigorates. A small moment of void, sustained. A small moment of emergence, and of formation. A resounding harmony within the body and mind, like that which bubbles in the core of the earth, is discovered when you delve into those depths.

Privacy, too, is silence. Don't look for attention, because the desire for it is a mistake. The more intimate a thing is, the more it should be guarded. Find comfort in privacy, and in what is shared with very few. Shed the need to be seen.

Silence is the perfect pair to uncertainty. When you are unsure what to say, say nothing. When you're unsure whether something is the truth, don't say it. Instead, learn, absorb, become. Listen for the truth in the cosmos. Seek it in the song of the spirit. Let silence be a warm blanket, and a comforting touch.

In silence, allow yourself to be seen. Allow yourself to go deeper. Hear the life that hides beneath the illusion of absolute quiet. The low hums and whirs and waves of what's around you.

And, once found, carry that silence with you. Keep it as a charm. If devices disturb the silence, hide them. If thoughts disturb the silence, quiet them. If there is no silence to be found, fill yourself with something fuller. Discover peace in the song of the spirit. Embrace all it can show you.

Because silence comforts the mind and eases the body. It allows the spirit to speak. Relish silence.

~

Resonance

Spirits have the gift of resonance. As one reverberates, as one shines, those around it, too, will shine. It's in this resonance that harmony is born. And in this way, spirits have the gift of communal music.

Resonance is something discovered. It is a well-played and well-timed note. A shared experience. Done well, it can be found in shared love, shared artistry, and shared joy. It can be found in shared creation and shared climax. But it is always shared.

Find in your own spirit that resounding note. And find resonance with those spirits whose resonant notes, combined with yours, create harmony.

Resonance is rare. Because while there is no limit to the number of people one could *find* resonance with, there is a sharp limit to the number of people one *will* resonate with.

But resonance, like all natural forces, does not limit itself to bodies. Discover resonance, first, with the cosmos. With the ground you tread and the murmur of life around you.

Seek resonance because from it spring joy, desire, and revelry. Because resonance reveals the body of god in all things. And because in it is the song of the spirit. Discovered and played well, this song harbors its own promise. And promise, lived, bears the overtones of harmony.

~

Harmony

Harmony is the truest state. In the spiritual cosmos, it is the equilibrium to which, in peace and fullness, all things settle.

It is, in this realm, harbored where life flourishes, wellbeing is bountiful, and health is collective. Harmony exists where deep truth is the first principle. Harmony emerges where shared love is the motivator.

Harmony is not made, but found. It is found in living with the cosmos, cycling with the earth, and singing with the spirit. It is found when you understand that your purpose is to live, and when you live this purpose well. It is found when you assume your role in the cosmic tapestry, and when you uplift others before yourself.

Harmony is all you want to be, could be, and would be. Harmony is in all you give and receive and share gratitude for. Harmony is empathy and mutual desire, the beauty of the whole self, well-tended, and the life that is full and deep and lasting.

Where there is health, it thrives, and where there is love, it lingers. It finds its contours in the resonance of spirits, and it blossoms in the deep well of the core of your soul. Harmony is an extant wave whose roots lie in the eons of past, in the ancient ages of the void into which life first burst, and whose branches stretch into the progeny of progeny, past a time when much of what's known would belie recognition. Harmony can be found in any place or time. It can be found by probing deeper, or shedding layers, or sharing truths. It can be found in all that is beautiful, and all that gives life, and all that lives.

Because harmony is the natural course of all things. Because harmony is the equilibrium to which all things stretch, and to which all things one day return.

Harmony is the cosmic cycle, and the reverberant truth. It is the waves of life that wash over you when you breathe, and when you laugh, and when you share touch. It is the fullness of the spirit that sings because it must, as birds do. That moves because it must, as seas do. That changes because it must, as earths do.

Harmony is not rushed or forced. Where there is rushing, there cannot be harmony. Where there is force, there cannot be peace.

Harmony is strong because it is gentle. It is beautiful because it lives. True because it belongs to the soul.

To live fully, purposefully, honestly—to be rooted—is to cultivate harmony in the world.

When you go into the world, consider: how are you contributing to its fullness?

Where are you falling into place, and where are you failing to?

How can you serve, in small and modest ways, but also larger ways, as the cosmos calls on you to?

Harmony is found in the way you relate to all that is. In each truth you accept and then live. In each moment, in each act of tending, and in each honest transformation.

To live by the song of the spirit is to cultivate harmony in your body, mind, and

155

world. And this is why you should give yourself to it. Because to give yourself to harmony
is to give yourself to life.

Live. And discover the harmony that all
life emerges from, discovers, and rediscovers.
Live and witness what all life returns to. What
life is. Live well to create harmony in the
world—and in what lies beyond it.

~

Movement

Ebb and flow. Rise and fall. Wax and wane and wobble.

All of life is movement.

The beating pulse and the rushing blood. The shifting skin and the shaking hair. Inching growth and throbbing twitch and the dance to find the perfect spot to lay in bed. Each of these tiny movements is a microcosm of the larger movement. The larger movement is life.

Even in stillness, there is movement. To sit perfectly still is to move against forces that would pull you out of stillness. It is a constant effort of muscles and bones. Movement is everywhere, in everything.

Harmony itself is the perfect movement of sounds and truths together.

This is why the mind and body, well-moved, become beautiful. Because they find in themselves a harmony. To move is to fill with life. When you feel in your body a need for movement, allow it to do so. With rhythm and difficulty, make a mantra of your body.

Breathe. Gesticulate. Exert and repeat. When you feel in the mind a need to wander, let it. Run away with it, and come back again. Give it the nourishment of deep thought and daydreams. Of rich conversation, and meditation. Let the mind live.

The spirit, too, moves. It moves in the depths of dreaming. It wanders with the hypnotic trickle of water, and it vibrates in the quiet hum of morning. In health and harmony, the spirit will soar. In truth, it will sing. If you let it, it will live.

Move with life.

~

Beauty

Beauty, at its truest, is the fullness of life, revealed. It is the perfect consequence of honesty. It is born of harmony, health, and movement. It discovers itself, in the creases of your skin, and the sound of your song. It dribbles with the sweat down your back, and weaves with the breeze through the pores of your skin. It swells with your chest, and it fills with your tears. It lives and it grows and it changes. It is never complete, and always present. It thrives in the organic. It is cultivated and sculpted—but never cut or refashioned. It is brought forth, not placed upon.

Beauty is the honesty at the heart of everything difficult, and the immodesty at the core of every desire.

Find it in the truth, and stay with it. Keep it. Let it grow as all living things seek to. Feed it and cultivate it and teach it. Empower it. Beauty is a force and a being. It does not like to be rushed. Coax it, instead. It likes to shine. Allow it to be bright.

To bring it out, move. With the beating pulse of the earth, and with the rhythm of change. Birth it with the chanting of your body. Keep it with ritual, and nurture it with *carefreedom*. Challenge yourself.

To create beauty is to grow and return to what was always there. To chisel away and to embrace. To birth and to release.

Beauty is not inherent. It is not affixed, or perfect. True beauty is not insertable, and it is not applicable.

Beauty is cultivated.

Beauty is honest.

Beauty is a way of life.

Be, always, beautiful.

~

Transcendence

Transcendence is a moment of flight. It is a heightening of awareness, a touching again that place from which you came, and to which you will return. A reconnection with the *all* of things. It is a beautiful part of a full life.

But too often, it becomes a goal. Too often, people will confuse the state of transcendence, the state of being in that place, with true awareness or understanding. But that is a mistake. You are here to live, not to escape life. If you were meant to be there, you would be. A bird flies and arrives back on land. A dolphin jumps and arrives back in the water. Remember, always to return.

Don't become lost in the search for transcendence. Do not seek false comfort in escaping the life you're here to immerse in, or accept the mistruth that transcendence is about you. Instead, understand transcendence for what it is: a momentary state, and a part of a whole life. Allow it to be a reminder of the cosmos within you, and the vastness of the cosmos around you.

And pursue, instead, immersion.

~

Immersion

Greater than transcendence, is immersion. To immerse is to be fully within the space in which you are called to be, in a given moment. It's to be pulled, by the lull of waves or song or truth, and to enter a deeper space, where the spirit lives. It is in this space that harmony is found.

To immerse is to meditate, and be fully with the cosmos. It is to pray, and be fully with the spirit. It's to live, and be fully in your life. In all cases, immersion is a channel for the emergence of the spirit into a place.

It is the ultimate presence, because it is a presence of spirit.

In daily life, it's usually discovered in absent-mindedness, sleep, or trance. It's most visceral in the early morning, by the waves or with the low, steady hums and whirs and white noise of a room, or the washing tides of the street outside.

It is possible to find transcendence, but not immerse. This is the mistake. Because transcendence is meant for a moment—like all natural states, it should not be permanent. In achieving it, seek to immerse yourself in the cosmos, even for those few moments. Follow where you're led and remain there.

In physical life, immerse yourself in what you are doing, by being fully present—mind, body, and spirit. These three will not be there all at once. Lose yourself a moment, and your spirit will shine through. Exert yourself, and your body is there. Think deeply, and without distraction, and your mind is there.

Immersion is a state of change, and evolution. It is a constant waxing and waning and coming and going. It is a rush of the waves. A run of the river. A beat in your heart.

It can be found in the climax of a song, or the words of a book. In the mantra-making of the body during conscious, rhythmic movement, and in the brightness of any moment that fills the heart. And it is always there in the truth of things. In the song of the spirit, deeply channeled. Root yourself in it, and you will feel immersion everywhere.

Live in truth. Immersion finds you, where you let it.

~

Honesty

Honesty is the key to the singing spirit.

To be honest is to live in truth. Not your truth. The truth. The deepest truth is not personal, and it's not individualized. It's constant, and it's eternal.

The deepest truth is peaceful, vibrant. It moves with, and not against, the cycles of life. It is cosmic. It comes with you into this world, and it goes and remains as you go and remain.

Be honest in the things you say, always. If you're unsure whether they're true, don't say them. Be honest in what you do, and in how you are. If it's too avoidant, don't do it.

Honesty is silence in the morning, and speaking softly through the day. Honesty is listening, just to listen. Honesty is being with, just to be with. And it is always there, ready to be held.

In immersion, and delving, and movement, you'll find honesty. You'll find it in the song of the spirit, the hum of the earth, the light of the moon. The pull of the stars.

Be always as you are meant to. Honest.
Harmonic. Alive and full.

Gratitude

Honesty is gratitude.

Gratitude is the recognition of all that you are given; breath in your bones, time to be different, beautiful things that inspire.

To be grateful isn't to be ignorant of desire. It's to be filled with desire for the gifts of life. It's to see the earth, your body, and the cosmos for all they are. It's to live in them fully. To place at their altar a small offering, and to partake in a deep act of reverence.

If you take part in no other rituals, embrace the ritual of gratitude.

~

9.
The hidden truths

✹

Some truths are hidden. In the deepest trenches of life. In the darkest shadows or most embarrassing things. And this makes them so much more important to uncover, understand, and embrace.

It's too often that people run from what's true simply because it is hidden. Or simply because it is vulnerable—or because it makes them feel vulnerable. And in doing so, they miss the light of knowledge, the spark of growth. The chance at communion.

So, if a truth makes you vulnerable, or if it is itself vulnerable, that's when you trust it even more. There is no wrongness in truth. And when the truth is hidden by darkness, by taboo, or by the visceral—then the darkness, the taboo, and the visceral are not things to be healed, but forces to be explored.

Because it's not only about the underlying truth. There is also, often, some beauty to the hiding places. Some fundamental aspect of a full life. A manifestation of the cosmic principles which call you always to be rooted in them.

So, don't accept that because something is dark or difficult, or scary and complex, that it therefore must be escaped.

Watch it and see what says.

Test the waters, and swim if it's right.

Dive into it, and retrieve what shines.

Because sometimes the vulnerable truth is the greatest truth of all.

~

Desire

So much of a society is a daily suppression of desire. Work when you want to play. Restraint when you want to indulge. Patience when you want it now.

And yet, desire can be a compass. Not absolute; indulgence should be careful. Patience should be practiced. Responsibility should be observed.

But desire *itself* is often a part of something deeper. It points you in the direction of what could be, and sometimes, what's still needed.

Because desire is a manifestation of a deeper truth. It is a foreigner, speaking in the language of your heart, but not the language you know. You may interpret desire's words in the way you understand—but they may not mean what you think they do.

Sometimes, you may hear junk food, when desire speaks of flavor, and nourishment. You may hear festivity, when desire speaks of comfort, company, intimacy. You may hear a specific career, where desire speaks of service and purpose. Often, in these moments, the two are not the same. And always, in these moments, the question is one of truth.

The truth is never ugly. The truth is never overindulgent. The truth is never artificial. The truth is breathing, and deep, and resonant. The truth of desire makes itself known when you truly listen. When you take stock of life. When you are guided not by aimless whims or musings or even the expectations of a society—but by the song of the spirit.

So, be guided by it. Indulge in it. Be true to it. And take the time, whenever you feel desire arising in you, to understand what it is saying. In its depths, you'll find honesty. In its depths, you'll find direction. Put into practice, cultivated with the foundation of health—being well in your mind, body, and spirit—and with the foundation of devotion, you will find harmony.

~

Intimacy

Understand that all acts of life are intimate acts. From the caress of wind on the skin to the sliding and weaving of waves on the body. From the nestle of a first embrace to the waking breath of a first morning. From the honest reflection to the careful confession. Life is an intimate force. So intimate, it lives within you, courses through you, and wraps around you.

Strange, then, that so much in societies is built to avoid intimacy. The separation of place, into workplace, living place, leisure place—when leisure and work are both embedded in life. Or the prescription of remedies to what are, effectively, manifestations of life. The careful crafting of sexless, dispassionate beings meant to produce without offense, and to engage without connection. The expectation that a society's people exist within a careful set of parameters meant to protect against messiness, emotion, and uncertainty.

But that isn't the full experience, and it isn't the full life. To build a society on the foundation of respect, compassion, and care isn't the same as building a society on foundations of separation, prescription, and mistruth. Because the truth is an intimate thing. Without intimacy, there cannot be honesty. Without honesty, there cannot be full life. Without full life and living, there cannot be harmony. And in a place where life is restrained as a matter of course, each participant feels it, somewhere. Each person forced to take part understands it, in some way.

Some may accept it or embrace it as fact—and that is a lived dishonesty that hurts the whole society.

The truth is in the free and intimate act, harmonized. The truth is in the whisper in the quiet, and the pull in the moment. The truth is in the comforting weight of trust, in the honest allure of possibility, and in the promise of what is.

And there is intimacy in truth.

Be cautious in who you are intimate with. Because intimacy imprints. And sometimes it swallows. Be intimate only with those you would have imprint on you. Be intimate only with what you would allow to swallow you whole. To be intimate is both to share in a great power, and to bow completely. It's not something to be done lightly. Because when it is, it is wasted. The spirit frays a little. The mind is sapped and the body sags.

So go forward, instead, with care. Be led by the call of the spirit.

Be intimate with yourself. Be intimate with others. Be intimate with life. With your heart, kiss what invigorates. With your mind, touch what mystifies. With your body, embrace who loves. Because the spirit is always intimate, and intertwined, with the threads of life. Its breath rises and falls with the tides and its movements pull and are pulled like the cosmos.

In this is the truest intimacy.

The intimacy that lives, and breathes, and sways. The intimacy that gives and is given and

given to. The natural intimacy of every day, of
always. The intimacy of the spirit.

Sex

Sex, at its truest, is a gift. The tracing of fingers on the skin, and the breath on the thighs. The cold fire that fills from the stomach to the fingertips. The fullness that twists, and glows, then erupts, and the waves that flow and conjoin and subsume.

Sex is an exploration of the body. Where deepened, it is a meeting of spirits. When it stems from desire, and is girded in devotion, it is profound, resonant, honest. It becomes the deepest movement, and it becomes the highest resonance.

Where there is no desire, and no devotion, there can be no sex. Intimacy is always the domain of the intimate, and the body is always the domain of the bearer.

Like love, sex morphs and is varied. It is a wild, living entity, to ride and follow, to learn and to guide. It lives in you, a while. It brings to life, and it shares in life, and it keeps alive. The best sex is symbiosis. It is the press of fingers on skin, and the push and pull of wetness, and lightness, and fullness. It is the rush and the damp and the cool air that winds in the absence of recent breath. It flows and converges and tastes of water and fire. It's the sparkle of lightning at the peak. Entwining branches and streams that slide against each other. The coursing climax that orbits in silence, until it plants itself beneath the heart and between the legs and in the ridges of the skin.

Climax is the gift of pleasure handed down to you by the earth itself. Hidden in the core, a building pressure, waiting to be released. Waiting to be the pool that erupts, and the truth that cascades. Discovered in art, and in ritual. In privacy, and in communion.

So, why abuse this gift, by ingesting things that would mimic its effects in the mind or disrupt the natural rhythms of the body, or by hiding it in shame, or sharing it with someone undeserving? Because sex is carnal, visceral—and it is cosmic, spiritual. Find it in art, ritual, privacy, and communion. In intimacy and in desire. In those your spirit knows are worthy of all of you. Or alone when you have yet to meet them. In truth.

When you doubt from where it comes, listen closely, look carefully. Hear it in the waves, as they rush with pleasure. See it in the volcano, as it erupts to rain molten stone, to give life in generations to come. Feel it in the rain, as it showers down. In the swirling steam of the tea kettle. In the tickling bubbles of the bath.

Don't convince yourself that sex doesn't matter, or that it is anything less than sacred, less than powerful, less than natural.

Sex is not a thing to run from. It's not a silly thing to ignore, or an insignificant thing given too much weight. It is a sacred thing of the earth, and a manifestation of everything. Honor it. Savor it. Indulge in it. And let it do so in you.

~

Delving

To delve is to go deeper into life. To excavate and rediscover the truth of you and the world and the cosmos. To delve is deep reflection, and contemplation. It is existence without walls or stipulations. It is the abandoning of false ideals or presuppositions. It is the embracing of life, not because you must, but because life embraces you.

To delve is to know the pain of suffering, and to go further into health. And once there, to find the comfort of pleasure, and fullness. To delve is to know pain in the mind, and to go further into truth. To know grief, and to discover, in its depths, life.

To delve is to be honest with all there is. It's to be real.

In delving, all that has always been remains, and all that could be is revealed. It's in the depths of life—in grief, in pleasure, in immersion—that what seems like mystery becomes easy to understand.

So, pursue life, and embrace health. Avoid poisons and substances that deceive the body, mind, and spirit. Protect what and who you cherish.

And when encountered organically, when it emerges in you, don't run from grief, or uncertainty. And don't run from pleasure, or immersion. Not when they're true.

Because to do so is to run from life. And your purpose is to live. Don't run from that sacred calling. Find yourself, your place in it. Embrace it. Delve into who you are, and who you can be. Into things as they are, and how they could be. And you'll always be ready for what's to come, because you'll always carry the truth of what is.

~

Anxiety

Anxiety is the friction that arises of its own accord. It's the reminder that you are the wilderness. It is the storm of fear and nerves that mounts, at times, to panic. And in this storm, like trees in a monsoon, as the earth is in a hurricane, the key is to be rooted. Because what is rooted will shake, and rattle, and loosen. It may rise and fall and be carried for a while. But its roots, and the earth they bind to—the earth they're wound in—remain.

Unrooted, you will be tossed around in the fury of your own insides. Grounded, you'll find safety. This is why it's important, in all things, to find first your roots.

Of course, this isn't a storm that always passes. Sometimes it lingers, and strengthens, and you find yourself carried from your roots. Let yourself, for a brief time, go. Let it carry you. Because this storm is a natural thing.

But when they whisper to you—and they will—when you hear them in the voice of someone else, in the comfort of a place, or in the base of your body—remember your roots.

Remember the truth of your breath. Because this breath is the truth. And the moments that left you, the thoughts that possessed you in worry and panic—those are the deception. The truth beneath them is the reminder of what matters. Of who matters. The reminder of comfort, and grounding, and love. Seek those, instead. Seek the damp and fertile truth that takes root beneath the worry, not the storm that emerged in its wake. Accept what is true: know that you are the whole part. Know that about you, there is cosmos. Know that about you, there is spirit. Fall into its arms. And live.

~

Despair

There is no heaviness like despair. Despair is a lonely tragedy. It's a vast expanse. Grey. Broken only by rivulets of black-red grief, and deep, rippling pools of heartache.

Despair is a thing that is felt, and a thing that is experienced.

But, large enough, it also becomes a place that is lived in: a cage, comforting and painful. Tenacious enough, despair becomes a being that lives inside you. One that metastasizes, and that morphs any moment into something tasteless—something shallow and empty next to its own shadowy, bottomless depth.

In the trenches of despair are born things. New ideas and understandings. But even these don't help its pain. Despair is not a darkness that gives. It is one that takes. It swirls and overpowers the organs and tissues and bones. It sucks in the light and cages the spirit. It presses on the chest and fogs the mind. In the end, despair is the black hole of the heart.

It is important to understand despair. To see that despair is not a teacher. Despair is also not something that can be healed, truly, by artificial means. Instead, despair is a warning. The mourning of the spirit. The crying out that the first flame, that deepest core of you, grows weary and malnourished. The promise to transform each living moment into a dying moment.

You cannot escape or overpower despair. You can try, and you will fail. Some succeed at numbing the experience, but this is treating the symptom, not the source. Some succeed at ignoring the experience, but this is to be sick every day. You can't escape it or overpower it. You can only move through it. You can only bear it in each breath and each moment. But the truth, in bearing it, is to understand how. How to make it a light thing, more feather than mountain. The truth, in moving through it, is how to move quickly, more flying than swimming.

Sometimes, despair is born of loneliness. Other times, from the grief of loss. But always, it breeds these things. And often, it does not arise from any discernible event or cause. Sometimes, it is simply the pain of the spirit.

So how do you bear it? How do you move through it?

First, is not alone. Where there are more hands to help you bear it, seek them. Where there are wings to help you fly, find them. Where you cannot seek or find them in the physical world, find them among the spirits. Where you cannot hear them, find them in these pages. The truth is, in despair, you never mourn alone. Eternity mourns with you.

In despair, what echoes from the heart is heard by the collective spirit. What then resonates in the collective spirit is understood by the cosmos. And what is understood by the cosmos pools and grows cold. With all this mourning about you, find the time to provide comfort. When you are in mourning, embrace that which mourns with you. Give it comfort, and it, too, will give comfort to you. Allow yourself to receive that comfort.

Sometimes, you may feel you need time with despair. That it's too soon to lift or to move through. Spend time with it, then. Stay a while. But don't allow it to grow so heavy, or so unmoved, that it crushes you.

Remember, your responsibility is not only to your own experience, but to that first great task you were given: to live. To live is your first calling. It is your first challenge. To uphold, honor, and cultivate life around you is a core truth of honest life. Few things crushed can live. So, sit beneath the weight if you must. Bear the grey. But move before you think you are ready. Because allowed to sit there, you will never be fully ready.

To move through despair, you must go deeply into it. You must be with it, truly. You must sit in its depths and allow yourself to mourn. You must allow yourself silence. You must allow yourself sobbing. You must allow yourself pangs and pity.

And then you must exhale. Collapse into the arms of love and comfort. And understand that those arms are cosmic arms. The eternal arms of god and spirit and life. Arms that always understand.

In those arms, find the space to be intimate, not clinical. And you will find they lift you a little. If you allow them to, you will rise, just enough to move. And as you begin to move, with time, you will find life coursing back into your body. You will feel the cycles of beginnings and swells and rebirths course through you. You will feel the chanting of the cosmos, and hear the coaxing, the cheering of the world of spirit. You will be, again, you.

And if you move still further, you will feel the warmth of life on the other side. The light of the sun. Here, return to the song of the spirit, and let it guide you through. Where there is no one else, it will always be there.

To bear despair, you must grow larger than it. You must sit and find that the truth is always larger than it. Realize that the truth of you is greater than your bones or heart or mind. That you are, and have always been, cosmic. That the cosmos have always imbued you. You must understand how small you are, one small wave in a drop within a wave, and how great it is to be so. Because that wave contains the ocean.

And in sitting with that knowledge, you allow the ocean to carry you. To be with you.

You allow all that is cosmic within you to glow. And here is where the icy weight of despair thaws, ever so slightly, but just enough to bear. Thawed in this way, you can welcome those same cosmic arms, this time, to help you lift.

And in so lifting, you may find a wholeness, a resplendence not there before.

You have grown.

This is why it's important not to run from despair, and not to seek it out. When it comes, be with it—but quickly dispose of it. Over time, with increased health, abundance, and intimacy, you will find that despair comes less and less frequently. You will find that, when it's coming, you can begin the process of making it light, before it even arrives. That once it arrives, it is like a feather. White. And with one puff, the feather will pass right over your head and settle back in the rhythm of the cosmos.

Allow yourself the freedom to be light. Allow yourself the freedom to be loved.

Because the deeper truth of life is not a mediation of despair, but a cultivation of gifts.

The deeper truth of life is an expression of cosmic purpose.

In this cultivation and in this expression, deeply held and amplified, you can find life's greatest gift: joy.

~

10.

Reaching the root

※

Deep in the halls of the chest, and just beyond it—deep within the depths of the churning cosmos, lies all that could one day be.

That spark and that void and their totality. That seed and that rhythm and its dance. That space and that fire. They are life. They are a reminder of the root that took and gave and takes and gives and that will, always.

Truth has never been a matter only of observation. Truth has always been about understanding. To understand the truth of things is to reach that root. To take to it and to reconnect with it and all it has to give. It is to shape and frame a home for the mind. To create a space to grow and shine. To allow for something that really isn't found anywhere else *but* in the cosmos. *But* in the natural. *But* in the spirit.

The return to center is a return to rooted-ness. We are here to be rooted, and to create rootedness. That rootedness is how to live, and why to live. It is a guide to where you're going, and where you could go, and where you should go. It is rebinding the thread between all life. It's embracing the natural. Accepting the cyclical and wading back into the cosmos that society has become so untethered from.

To be rooted is to stop spiraling away, and to understand instead the spiral of all things. It is to cycle with. To know cosmic rhythms, and subtle rhythms. It is to create heaven, for you and the world. For selves and worlds to come.

Rootedness is something to be born into. Every day and in every moment. Rootedness is something to return to and to excavate and to create. Rootedness is a state of being to envelop yourself in. It is a way to become *you*. Again. Always.

So, root yourself.

Become.

192

Because the key to living is in the two together.

~

Faith and Knowing

The spirit is not a thing to be believed in. It is a truth to be known.

What you read here is not an idea. Like god, like water, it isn't a metaphor, and it isn't a question of faith. It is a deep knowing. An understanding. An awakening.

To know the spirit, is to close your eyes and move. To sit by the water and listen. To know with your heart, and trust with your mind.

To know god is to stand by the sea and look out. To reflect on the canopy in an ancient forest. It is to learn history, biology, physics, and witness the bonds that unite all things. To consider what so many will choose to dismiss.

This is why it doesn't matter what you call them; spirits, the one that is you and the ones that are not, are here and there without your permission. It doesn't matter what you think of god; god is here, without your permission. And the living, cosmic ocean from which you came is the same ocean through which you live now, and to which you will return. When you return light, with harmony, justice, and love, it grows brighter, fuller. When you arrive heavy, with violence, dissonance, and pain, it grows dimmer, and an ugly note is struck across the cosmos, across all time and space. It leaves a scar to be healed. When you arrive too heavy for the light, for that ancestral sea of sun, you are unable to enjoin with it. When you return, instead, as you belong, the sea parts and welcomes you. A harmonic chord is struck. What is in this realm, flourishes as it does there. And the cycle continues.

People look for evidence of the spirit because they become numb to truth. Because they cannot see the evidence right in front of them. Cannot feel the evidence that courses through them. People grow and they know pain, and they forget how to feel. People come to believe they have heard everything, and forget how to listen. They forget how to look, and really see.

They become enmeshed in self-righteous dogmas—secular as often as otherwise—and with these, wrap themselves in a blanket of superiority. And when they do, they rob themselves of the opportunity to *understand*. Because it doesn't only matter what you believe; it matters what you know. It matters that you understand what's *true*.

People ask, "how can there be good, when there is evil?" They ask, "who could allow this to happen?" And when they do, they miss the truth completely. Because the world of spirit does not exist to play out their beliefs. If there is goodness in a place, it is because the society is good. If there is malice in a place, it is because the society is malicious. And yes, in any society, you will find goodness *and* malice. Just as in the world of spirit, you will find weight and lightness, harmony and discord. This is the point. The world of spirit works through this one. And that is why you exist. Why all exist. We live here and touch it, just as it lives there and touches here. We return to it with the weight or the weightlessness of this place, and our roles in it.

It is nature, of the highest kind. It is truth, of the deepest sort. It is the cosmos. It is the cycle. And the cycle continues.

So, understand this: all of creation is the evidence. Life is the evidence. God is the evidence. There is no trick to be witnessed, to make a person believe. There is no miracle to be spun, upon which to claim validity. The trick is life. The miracle is you.

It is exactly because so many cannot see the miracle of themselves that they refuse to see the miracle of the earth. And it is because people cannot see the miracle of the earth that they refuse to see the miracle of the spirit.

Over time, so many have twisted the ideas of god and the spirit to confuse, to violate, and to wage war. The god you've heard of—that is not the god that exists. The god that exists is no one thing. God is greater, always. And god does not belong to us. We belong to god.

Don't build worldviews on faith. *Know* the truth. Don't go having faith in yourself. *Know* yourself. Don't just believe in others. *Know* others.

It's not about belief or faith. It's about rediscovering. Seeing the world for what it is, and the cosmos for what they are. It's about knowing.

There is no complexity to knowing. There is ignorance, and there is dismissal. Or there is opening the eyes and seeing what is. When you are honest, and humble, you will know. When you are truthful, and reverent, you will see. And when you learn, commune, and live well, you will understand. To know the spirit is the greatest gift of all. All are born with it. Many forget. But you can always remember. You can always look again.

Because what is there does not forget you. And what is there always sees you.

See it back. Honor it back. Love it back.

~

Thinking in Lifetimes

When you're uncertain, or when you have choices in front of you, remember to think in lifetimes.

Not in five-year plans or in temporary feelings. In *lifetimes*.

In this lifetime, how would you feel if you didn't choose it? When it's ending, would you regret never having discovered what was on the other side of it? Not having tried?

In this lifetime, how would you feel if you did? When it's ending, will you wish that you'd done something different?

Move your mind through time. Seek to understand not only what you desire, but what your life will miss, or gain. Consider that time, itself, is a useful illusion. That this *moment* is pregnant with every moment there ever was, and every moment there will ever be. That each moment contains the whole of life.

Trust what is honest. Seek to understand what a desire, fear, or frustration is *really* telling you. Because this lifetime, like every lifetime, is a gift, and it is a charge. Don't squander it in disservice to those around you. Don't waste it denying what could be, or disrespect it by not caring for it properly. Live it fully. Live it well. And allow its magnitude, its eternity, to guide your choices. This lifetime is a universe. It is a tiny focal point in the cosmic tapestry, and a hanging thread that wonders if it'll be stitched as it asks to be, or forgotten and left fraying.

To think in lifetimes is to stitch the thread.

~

Birth

Begin again. This is the truth of all things. In its purest form, life does not begin or end, it is conferred. When you come into this world, you emerge from the place to which you will return. The body is the merging of DNA, the forming of earth and flesh and fibers into a unique new mold. Like the body, the spirit is the shaping of cosmos, the movement of soul and waves and music into its own unique mold. When your body's base particles, the cells, cease their endless cycle, it is ready to return to the earth. But the spirit remains, a while. When the spirit's tides and memory grow distant and it is also light with peace, it is stripped to its own base particle— soul—and returns to that great sea of life. And somewhere, someday, a being is born.

Because to die is to return there, and to be born is to return here. And each day is that birth. Each day is the moment to begin again. But some births are greater than others. And the greatest birth is the birth into the truth. The birth of the song of the spirit. It is not only to seek, or to do—but to become. From your core to your fingertips. From your body to your spirit. To embrace the truth is to begin again. To be with the song of the spirit is to live for the first time. Born into it, live only this life. The life of harmony, and beauty, and truth. Be full of it. Be full in it. And you will be complete. You will find it is that ultimate, sacred thing: purpose.

~

The spiral of everything

To live is to move through cycles. It's that rising, cycling, setting sun. That moon break, moon phase, and moon fall. The spinning earth and its rushing tides. The kissing breeze and the tickling river. That fourfold changing, growing, living. And the way they each exist in the rise and fall of your chest, the opening and closing of your pores, the flows of your body.

And there is a secret in this cycle. One paramount truth invisible when you look only with eyes, and not the spirit. When you hear only with the ears, and not the heart. It was, for the people of the first way, a simple and hidden knowledge.

And that is this: the cycle is not an endless circle. It is a spiral. It begins at the center, and grows, and grows, until it reaches an expanse beyond the view of those within it.

You can find this truth in the moon, that grows, slowly, painstakingly, farther from the earth. You can see it in the earth, as its ellipsis grows, slowly, farther from the sun. You will see it in the galaxies the permeate this universe. And you will see it in this universe, beginning from a point, and spiraling outwards, at times and in places enfolding and interweaving with itself.

Stars, too, rise in this way. Expanding until they can expand no more, or exhaling and shrinking down.

The greatest spirits—the brightest, fullest, harmonic spirits, of great teachers and guides, of those who have lived many cycles and become a living conduit, or a great ancestor— these spirits, too, move this way. Expansive, spiraling outwards, a presence quickly felt.

And in the same way that spirit mimics star, body mimics earth and moon. The living bodies of a planet are gifted with expansion and contraction, as the various forces of the physical realm pull on them. The embryo that expands into body. The body that expands into adulthood. The adult that contracts in old age. But when it returns to the earth, it begins a new cycle. It grows large again, in the fertile soil, and in the trees. And one day, when the earth too nears the end of its cycle, it will find a new form, full with the bodies of all that have shared in its shelter, and larger than before. The life that courses through each person and the mind that sparks within them each expand and spiral outwards, until they stretch so far they seem to dissipate. And the spirit, once it is ready to return to the place from which it came, conjoins and becomes large again, in losing itself.

God, too, spirals, through all the life that dots the cosmos. Permeating, imbuing, and surrounding. Giving lifeblood. In the realm of spirit, and in the living energy that births all life, finding within itself new gifts to give. Imbuing skin with breath, and making clay of cells. And it is right that it should be this way.

Because the spiral is the truth of the wind. It is the twining of the heart about itself in grief and desire. It is the core of the self in life and in memory. The spiral is the story you were given before you were born, and the principle that will remain in your next movements. It binds all beings and births all love. Of harmony, it is the root melody. Adorn yourself in it. Live in it. Find it wherever you look, but look always with more than the eyes. Read it in these pages, and sing it in your life and mind. Discover it in those resonant spirits you are gifted to encounter, and within all you are called to love. Discover it within yourself, and should you ever forget it's there, look to the earth, and look to the sky. Keep it secret when you must, but keep it always. And when time passes, turn again to the song of the spirit. Begin again.

Because in you is the wholeness of the universe. In you is life, and movement, and truth. And in the universe is you. In society is you. Don't underestimate this expansive and limitless life—it is the gift of the cosmos. It is harmony, and the deepest truth. It is the love of the sun, and the warmth of the water. It is the coolness of breath, and it's the fullness of touch. It is all there ever was, and all there will be. Honor it, always. Live it, always.

This is what it is to live deeply.

~

My Own Gratitude

*

Para minha Avó.
To everyone who is Beloved.
To everyone who is Family.
To everyone this touches.

To you.

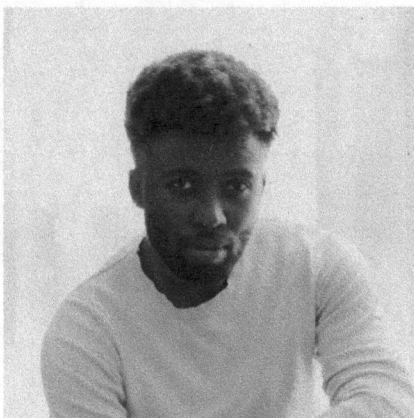

About the author

*

In an era where meaning is hard to come by, Pedro Tofua offers something more.

A lifelong writer, Pedro believes everyone is called to live deeply. His work explores the roles of history, the present, the natural, the physical, the spiritual, the social, and more in making the realities we live in. It is rooted in the ancient, living philosophies of southern Africa, and grounded in the tremendous power of life, and the spirit, to transform the world. This is his first book.

For more, head to pedrotofua.org

www.ingramcontent.com/pod-product-compliance
Lightning Source LLC
Chambersburg PA
CBHW010330030426
42337CB00026B/4882